GAME-TIME
DECISION
MAKING

*High-Scoring Business Strategies from
the Biggest Names in Sports*

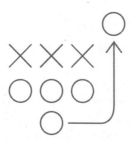

DAVID MELTZER

NEW YORK   CHICAGO   SAN FRANCISCO   ATHENS   LONDON   MADRID
MEXICO CITY   MILAN   NEW DELHI   SINGAPORE   SYDNEY   TORONTO

1 2 3 4 5 6 7 8 9   QVS   24 23 22 21 20 19

ISBN 978-1-260-45261-7
MHID 1-260-45261-1

e-ISBN 978-1-260-45262-4
e-MHID 1-260-45262-X

Library of Congress Cataloging-in-Publication Data

Names: Meltzer, David C., author.
Title: Game-time decision making : high-scoring business strategies
    from the biggest names in sports / David Meltzer.
Description: New York : McGraw-Hill, [2019]
Identifiers: LCCN 2019010733 (print) | LCCN 2019012476 (ebook) |
    ISBN 9781260452624 () | ISBN 126045262X () |
    ISBN 9781260452617 (alk. paper) | ISBN 1260452611 (alk. paper)
Subjects: LCSH: Decision making. | Strategic planning.
Classification: LCC HD30.23 (ebook) | LCC HD30.23 .M455 2019
    (print) | DDC 658—dc23
LC record available at https://lccn.loc.gov/2019010733

McGraw-Hill Education books are available at special quantity discounts to use as premiums and sales promotions or for use in corporate training programs. To contact a representative, please visit the Contact Us pages at www.mhprofessional.com.

To my beautiful wife, Julie, and my M&Ms—Marissa, Mia, Marlena, and Miles—as well as anyone else who should be acknowledged . . . especially my mom!

Contents

Foreword

Whe I first met David Meltzer, I was simply excited to discuss my new book *Shut Up and Listen!* about the hard truths that drive success; and yet I actually learned that David and I had a lot in common. David had excelled in the technology space early in his career and found equally as much success (or more) as a sports executive. He came to my office to record an episode of his popular podcast, *The Playbook*, where I shared some of my philosophies and strategies that helped me build my multibillion-dollar hospitality empire: Fertitta Entertainment, Landry's Inc., Golden Nugget Casinos and Hotels, and the NBA's Houston Rockets. I learned that David had also built an empire, lost it, but eventually built another. What struck me upon my initial meeting with David was a simple phrase that we both believe in, a phrase that I would say is the key to *Game-Time Decision Making*: "Get out of your own way."

The countless successes I've had over my career, which have also afforded me the dream opportunity to buy my hometown Houston Rockets franchise, all boil down to the ability to make consistent and efficient decisions. So many of us get in our own way and prevent ourselves from reaching our potential that we tend to be our own worst enemies, especially those of us who resist change. Having the awareness and mindset to make the right decision is what separates the biggest names in sports and business from the rest. It's the difference between great athletes such as James Harden and the twelfth man on an NBA roster, or between Warren Buffett and pretty much everyone else. Those who can make tough calls (and be right), no matter how critical the situation, are those who will win. When you can make intentional decisions with consistency, you will succeed more often than not, and that approach pays off in the long run with big wins!

No matter what "game" you're playing, teaching others to make the right decisions is even more important for leaders. If you can equip others with the ability to make informed and well-reasoned calls, your impact is scalable. This is the core of David's approach to *Game-Time Decision Making*: to empower you and those around you with the awareness and ability to make the right call when the "game" is on the line and the pressure is high.

I've always said that in order to thrive as a business leader you need four core fundamentals: a great product, an understanding of your financials, a good grasp on operations, and the ability to sell and market your business. The ability to choose the right path, take the right risks, and implement the new skills or knowledge you gain along the way is solely dependent on your decision making. This begs the question: "How can we set ourselves up for successful decision making?" Realize your talents, gifts, and competencies, and determine how those show a clear path to making money or not.

Letting your talents guide your path is a strategy that paid off for me personally. As a young child, I didn't watch cartoons, instead preferring to "play business" by carrying a briefcase (and a dealmaking attitude) with me. I carried that knack with me as I grew, eventually building a multibillion-dollar organization from an initial $6,000 loan when I was in my early twenties. I have seen the business world evolve since building my first hotel in Galveston in 1986, and I know that those who embrace change and display a willingness to grow will always be the individuals who achieve the greatest heights. The phrase, "we've always done it that way," is never a good explanation or justification. Even if 95 percent of your business is "perfect," working on that remaining 5 percent is essential. You need to place greater importance on embracing change in order to stay in the game and win in the long term. Of course, there is always a need to make big decisions when there is change occurring.

The strategies that David outlines in his book will empower you to make the right calls in *your* life, providing you the tools to outsmart and outwork others, while also bringing the right people along with you. Nothing happens accidentally, so be intentional in your decision making and embrace the need to change and grow, so that you will succeed every day of your life as you learn from David's *Game-Time Decision Making* strategies!

—Tilman Fertitta

Introduction

T he premise behind this book is simple: learn to be prepared to make decisions in the moment with confidence, clarity, balance, and focus.

The world's best coaches and managers make a living being confident that they have the right information to make the best decisions—and you should as well. No matter what pressure you might feel when forced to make tough calls, you can develop the awareness you need to make the right choices, time after time. You can learn to let the choices you have made in the past inform the calls you make in the future, without losing sight of the present. You can prepare yourself for the next game with consistency and persistence as you cultivate a ceaseless drive to be a more effective leader capable of unsurpassed decision making.

Throughout a career spanning nearly four decades, working in technology, sports, media, and entrepreneurship, alongside so many exceptional individuals, I've seen firsthand the strategies that have helped all of those who live with the spirit of excellence achieve success and turn their wildest dreams into reality. From the Silicon Valley boom to the NFL Draft busts, I've seen the highs and lows of what the sports and business worlds have to offer, and those experiences have afforded me the opportunity to observe and learn from unbelievable people who carry the spirit of excellence, from Hall of Fame athletes, coaches, and trainers from all different sports to billionaires, entrepreneurs, real estate moguls, technology pioneers, Silicon Valley mavericks, countless self-made entrepreneurs, speakers, inventors, and thought leaders.

I have leveraged the mentorship I gained from those people, whether it was gained by watching them, working with them, or simply asking for their help. It has informed my unique perspective and allowed me to design a philosophy built around the core tenets of decision making.

When I was a college athlete, I played football against future NFL players, like the "Nigerian Nightmare" Christian Okoye, who I like to say gave me my first autograph when he ran me over and left a cleat impression on my chest. As a sports agent and CEO of Leigh Steinberg Sports & Entertainment, one of the most notable sports agencies in the world, I learned the ins and outs of the sports industry.

From the beginning, I have always loved looking at decision making through the lens of sports, and in business, as in sports, it often comes down to split-second decision making "on the field," when the game is on the line, when the pressure is on, and your whole team is counting on you. Sports and business are both arenas where understanding yourself is just as important as understanding your opponent, where to be a winner and to create a dynasty of achievement and success, you need to make consistent decisions in an efficient, effective, and statistically successful manner.

Consistency, whether in life, on the field, or in the boardroom, comes from a combination of factors. The first of these is your awareness, which means having a clear understanding of the given situation, picturing desired outcomes, and acting accordingly. Decisions are also influenced by your conviction in achieving your goals and by the core values you hold, which inspire you to keep pushing through any adversity and curbing any inclinations to quit.

You must also be able to access the information you need rapidly, accurately, and with confidence, while also detaching your emotions from the desired outcome. The final component of consistent decision making comes from approaching each new game-time decision with a mindset of desire that strives for greatness, what I call a *spirit of excellence*, along with the equally important aspect of forgiveness. You must understand that not every decision you make will be correct, and that's OK. There is never an acceptable excuse to stop making those calls, however.

This book is organized into different areas of focus to help you make expedient and effective decisions in your life. Each chapter starts with a brief introduction, similar to a walkthrough or pregame analysis in sports terms, and it concludes with a postgame wrap-up to review and reaffirm the strategies that were shared in the chapter. The tools enclosed will prepare you to make the right calls when you face tough decisions, but my aim is also to help you gain what you need to position yourself to execute on the decisions that you make.

You'll learn how to build a team you can count on, a team that is united in its goals and values, willing to push themselves to be their best until the proverbial final whistle blows; how to build coaching trees; how to ensure that your past experience doesn't interfere with your future success; and how to devise successful marketing and branding strategies—lessons I have learned over many years in the business. But most importantly, this book will give you an opportunity to build your mindset, to become the type of leader and coach that you want to be: a person who will put his or her team in a position to excel no matter what game you're playing.

Enjoy the pursuit of your potential as a decision maker and leader, live with the spirit of excellence, and enjoy this book as you work toward the inevitable greatness that lies ahead of you.

1

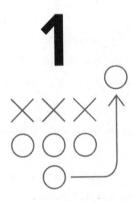

Putting Together Your Roster by Building Yourself

PREGAME ANALYSIS

A quarterback cannot be victorious if he has no one to throw to or hand the ball off to. No pitcher can win a game without run support and a strong defense behind them. Even the greatest basketball players in the world would be woeful playing one-on-five. Every great coach needs a team to lead. How should you approach building yours? Start from a strong foundation, with core values, friends, and family members who drive you forward in your goals.

Having a set of principles and standards will attract the right team members, and it will also empower you to cut ties with associates who aren't a great fit. It will prepare you to foster beneficial relationships with family, friends, and business associates while also developing a strong roster of mentors. Values-based leaders are prepared to make accurate and effective decisions, and they are ready for any test their industry throws in their direction. In the toughest situations, values-based leaders can lead their teams to win even when they have lost their star players.

Building yourself into a leader who inspires others to follow is no simple task, however. The best leaders have a firm grasp on the values that they believe in, and those values are what resonate most when building relationships, both in business and in life. As the head of an organization, you must also learn to listen to the input of others, filter advice in order to gain a better awareness of your surroundings, and leverage that heightened awareness to improve your decision making.

This chapter is designed to identify the role that leaders' values play in their recruitment of a winning team, how they can strengthen those values in order to identify the right players for their squad, and then the process of maintaining and growing those relationships.

Both personally and professionally, your having the knowledge to choose which relationships to build and which to sever is key to your success. Likewise, understanding how to deal with the advice you get from those around you is also important. With strong foundational values, an understanding of the worthwhileness of your relationships, a mindset that always seeks positivity, and an ability to deal effectively with difficult people, you will become a leader capable of constructing a dream team of your own.

ATTRACTING THE RIGHT PEOPLE TO OUR TEAM

To recruit the best players to our roster, it is essential that we develop and maintain meaningful relationships with the people surrounding us. But, ironically, the most important relationship we must develop and maintain to build our roster is with ourselves. We must not only think, say, and do the right things to attract the right people. We must also believe the right things and even carry the right energy. This can happen only if we create the right personal and team values: *gratitude*, *empathy*, *accountability*, and *effective communication*. After we learn to love ourselves, the people we surround ourselves with will become relative to our integrity, happiness, and energy—and so our bonds will strengthen.

Our dream team includes family, friends, associates, and mentors. And the key to developing and maintaining the right relationships with these people is understanding *relativity*.

What do I mean by "relativity"? I mean that everything and everyone on earth are all on the same team, no matter what. This understanding of relativity is meant to give you a perspective that is based on gratitude and empathy, which, in turn, makes everything relative to you. If you're always gracious, then everything is relatively good all the time. A grateful person sees that cup as nearly full, and an ungrateful person sees it as nearly empty. Legendary basketball coach John Wooden included a great aphorism in his 1973 book, *They Call Me Coach*: "Things turn out best for people who make the best of the way things turn out." Without the relativity that gratitude provides, we feel cheated, and we see only voids, obstacles, and shortages. With gratitude comes togetherness and a sense of team.

In building the right roster, we must start with those most relative to us: our team, our "position group"—that is, our peers—and our family. We must be aware of what our family members' intentions are so that we can surround ourselves with the best of our family members. Our DNA and our ancestral beliefs are why our families are most relative to our lives. This relativity gets even more complex for people who are part of a family, organization, or friend group with highly dysfunctional aspects and behaviors.

For example, what if you were born into a family with an extremely abusive, alcoholic father? How would you deal with a situation like that? Or if a sibling were physically or emotionally abusive? We can find ourselves falling into codependent relationships because we have no choice but to interact with the negative family members. This occurs in teams of all kinds, with discontent and negativity causing issues that limit overall success.

A toxic member of the team whose values are not aligned can throw off the entire group. Although it can be difficult to sort out the emotional feelings we have toward our families or other people, I have learned over the years to consciously interact with only the people who clearly have my best interests in mind. Notice I said *consciously* interact with only the people who clearly have my best interests in mind. When we recruit our dream team, we must search for the people who have a positive effect on our conscious and subconscious mind. The people who have influenced our beliefs may not be near us physically, and they may no longer even be living, but we still need to combat any negative influences that we consciously (or subconsciously) experience.

We must also develop our roster of thoughts, treating each day as if we were a wheeling, dealing general manager (GM) on the first day of free agency or on the day of the draft. We need to evaluate the value that our thoughts, both new and repetitive, bring to our conscious and subconscious mind, just as GMs look at their talent. Are your thoughts providing you the necessary confidence or value? Or are you wasting time and energy on those thoughts needlessly? If the new or repetitive thoughts are not valuable, then cut them the way you would cut underperforming players. You want your thought roster to bring you as much value as possible, empowering you as you chase after your goals.

A lot of these valuable thoughts come from our dream team (the people around us), and that is why we must recruit the people to our dream team both in our conscious world, through our direct actions, and through our subconscious belief system—that is, the values and energy that we lead with. The functional definition of the word **recruitment** is the action of finding new people to support a cause. The best recruiters in sports tend to have a great track record of personal success, and they also foster development among their team members. They push their team members to be their best selves, on *and* off the field.

> RECRUITMENT: Just how important is recruiting when it comes to leading a winning organization? Nick Saban's dominating run as the head football coach for the University of Alabama demonstrates the advantages of high-level recruiting practices, with five national championship wins due, in large part, to a string of seven straight number one–ranked recruiting classes.

At its core, recruitment means to ask for help. Asking for help or advice from those team members most relative to us is an important part of building the best roster. But we must be careful about whom we take advice from and which advice we take. When loved ones give me advice, I take it as if I were grabbing a handful of sand. I am grateful for the advice anyone gives me . . . but . . . I sift through it and put into practice only the occasional pearls of wisdom I find. Remember, just because someone loves us doesn't mean they give us good advice.

PROCESSING ADVICE FROM OTHERS

When people give you advice on the decisions you make as their leader or colleague, it's important to always be gracious, simply for the fact that if they care enough to offer help, you should be grateful for their *intent*. However, these people, although they may be most relative to you, may not truly know what's best for you. They may give you bad advice, criticism, hurtful comments, attacking thoughts, or in extreme cases, all of those.

Your family members may think they know what's best for you, but their actions and thoughts basically generate from a belief that they've had more experience than you. Yes, they are your family, but in some instances, they can be the most damaging people in our lives, and they can do the most harm. No one has more kind or unkind opinions than your family, simply because they're most relative to you. Sigmund Freud has explained it this way: "I cannot think of any need in childhood as strong as the need of a father's protection."[1] There is an emotional element in your family relationships. You can't always apply rationality to your relationship with your mother and father because they are the most relative to you.

When your values have positioned you to be a leader of others, you must place a focus on the character of the individuals that you bring onto your team and consider whether their values and goals are aligned with yours. Those closest to you produce the most meaningful relationships. In football, the defensive players tend to be closest with other defensive players, the offensive players stick together, and the special teamers tend to be further removed from the other units.

The power of this relativity is why you have to consciously think about and separate yourself from the wrong people, even if they are like family. However, this doesn't mean that if you're unhappy with a member of your unit, you need to remove yourself from the situation immediately. We don't have to physically separate ourselves from anyone; there are some people we are forced to be around even if they don't make us feel good. They are certain family members, neighbors, business associates, schoolmates, teachers, and others. We separate ourselves from them by shifting the paradigm. We don't physically remove ourselves. We actually connect to them by being gracious and empathetic.

When I say "separate yourself," what I mean is this: you must believe in yourself and respond to their criticism with kindness. Another way of explaining the principle is this: you must be proud of your relationships. Embrace the team that you're on or work to find another squad. Even in a complex or dysfunctional situation, make all relationships meaningful by finding at least one positive attribute, even if it is remote.

For example, let's say you are a teenager and your dad often gives you bad advice or is overly critical. You don't have to pack up and leave. Instead, listen to what he says, but take the advice or criticism as if you grabbed a handful of sand. Be grateful that he at least cares enough to give you advice, but let the advice fall through your fingers graciously until you find a valuable grain or a pearl to hold on to. Next, you should forgive him because he is only projecting his own insecurities onto you. Gratitude and forgiveness will allow you to develop the roster for your dream team while also creating healthier relationships with the troublemakers and malcontents around you.

I'd like to believe all the advice I give my kids is worth holding on to, but I know that is not always true. And it would be nice to have to dispense advice only when I'm at my best because I definitely don't want to be advising someone when I'm at my worst.

We want to consider others with the same respect that we would like in return, even in those difficult situations when we feel as if we don't receive enough respect.

When I moved from San Diego to Orange County, just a mere 60 miles from where I grew up, one of the best things about the move was that it gave me more control over recruiting my new roster. I had lived in San Diego for so long with an extended family, many friends, and business associates, that it seemed I was unable to go anywhere without running into somebody who knew me or someone in my family who thought either too highly or too lowly of me. The people who thought too highly of me had seen me only at my best; those who thought too lowly of me had seen me only at my worst. That's why these family relationships are so complex: they know so much about you.

Some of these people think that we are always as they perceive us to be, based on a "snapshot" view of their own limited experience with us. Or even worse, they judge us solely based on what they have heard about us, good or bad. There is no gratitude, forgiveness, or empathy. This is certainly true when it comes to free agent athletes, who are always viewed through a lens of their past actions and transgressions.

One of my favorite examples of how to persevere through this judgment comes from US soccer legend Brandi Chastain. After making the World Cup team in 1991, a team that would win the first-ever championship, most would assume that her spot on the roster was safe, especially given her seven goals scored that season. However, she was cut in 1993 and missed out on the 1995 World Cup, which forced her to completely reevaluate her standing in the American soccer landscape. Dealing with the negative perspectives that coaches might have had about her, which had led to her being cut previously, she decided to demonstrate that their snapshot was incorrect through her *actions*. Chastain showed a willingness to play whatever position the coaches thought best, and in 1996, she proved herself beyond a measure of a doubt and made the squad, and she was eventually selected to take the world-famous 1999 World Cup–winning penalty shot.

You will, of course, likely come across this in both your business or personal realms. When I put on my first 50 For 50 Gala, one of the 50 "birthday" celebrations I held to raise money for the Unstoppable Foundation, I overheard one of my uncles thinking out loud, "I wonder how much David is getting paid for this?" At first it really hurt, and I felt like I didn't want my uncle on my team. I had worked so hard to plan 50 parties to raise money for an empowerment center in Kenya. I had sacrificed so much time and energy for others, and yet my uncle thought I was being selfish. It took me a moment to calm down, but I forgave him because his snap-shot of me, based on our history together, made him skepti-cal of my intentions. I used to be selfish, like that guy playing pickup basketball who acts like he's Kobe Bryant, instead of the giving person I perceive myself as today, and so his nega-tive perception was very understandable.

Sometimes the opposite situation occurs, and you are showered with adulation, even if you don't deserve it. This can be just as dangerous.

You mustn't take any vituperative thoughts to heart, and you mustn't let praise go to your head. You need to have gratitude, empathy, and forgiveness, and you need to for-give yourself for the lowest moments in your life and not give yourself too much credit for any of your accomplish-ments. Be humble in victory and defeat. Be proud of your life-affirming relationships, and do your best to recruit your team, filling it with gracious, loving, and forgiving people.

To achieve your championship wins, it is essential that you develop and maintain meaningful relationships. And the first meaningful relationship you must develop and maintain is the one with yourself. You must be accountable and honest to attract the right people. This can happen only if you live by the Four Great Truths (which are also the pillars of hap-piness): *gratitude, empathy, accountability*, and *effective com-munication*. After you learn to love yourself, everyone else becomes relative to your integrity, happiness, and energy. Then, your connections to others become stronger, and you deepen those connections through conscious effort.

When I travel with my wife, for example, she remembers everything we see—every church, painting, and restaurant. I tend to remember just the people. I believe the more people I meet and remember, the more ability I have to attract the right people and add them to my team. What am I looking for? Most important to me are gratitude, empathy, and an attitude of abundance. Do they behave like there is more than enough to make everyone happy, or do they live in a world of "just enough" or "not enough"?

Let me share a story that changed my perspective on filling my roster. As you may have experienced, when you have your first baby, it can be scary—like a case of dynamite that is leaking nitroglycerin. When your first baby is born, it is one of the greatest moments of your life. When we had our oldest daughter Marissa, what came to me at the moment when they handed me that baby was, "Holy shit . . . I don't know what I'm doing. I don't want to leave the hospital." I asked the head nurse if we could stay at least another day. The nurse regarded me with a **majesty of calmness** as I was holding this tiny five-pound, one-ounce little girl, looking terrified. The nurse let out a chuckle and shared the best parenting advice I have ever received: "All you have to do is love that little baby girl. That's all!" Suddenly, I knew my role. My job was simply to love this little girl! And I did. In fact, by the time my fourth child was born, I was such a grizzled veteran, my agenda was to leave the hospital ASAP. We actually snuck out of the hospital after only 17 hours. All my fear was gone.

> **MAJESTY OF CALMNESS:** A majesty of calmness comes from understanding your values and capabilities, which provides you the confidence to execute quick and successful decision making.

Our job is simple: love our family and love those who are most relative with us. Share with them gratitude and empathy, without an expectation of receiving those in return. Celebrate the uniqueness of others. See the big picture—a baby is born, a family member passes away, laughter echoes, tears are shed, but the legacy of your family lives on. The family is one of nature's most important works. George Santayana said, "The family is one of nature's masterpieces."[2] All the good and bad are relative things, so surround yourself with the right people in your family as often as possible.

PICKING THE RIGHT PARTNER

One of the most relative and important relationships that we must maintain is that of marriage or intimate partnerships. I feel sorry for couples who don't understand the spiritual side of intimacy or relativity. They're missing out. Like everything else, intimacy is a gift from Goodness to be opened at just the right time. "There is no more lovely, charming, and friendly relationship, communion, or company than a good marriage,"[3] said Martin Luther. That's why I believed my grandfather wholeheartedly when he told me there were only three things you needed to be happy in your life:

1. Find a job that you love. You spend a third of your life working. Do what you love to do, and the money will come. I can give you a thousand examples of people who started out in a profession they loved—whether they wanted to be an artist, musician, teacher, coach, quarterback—and then the money came.

2. Find the right partner or spouse. You spend a third of your life with your family, and as I've said earlier, your family members are the most important and most relative people in your life. You need to find the right person to share your life with. Find that right woman or man; find that intimate companion. He or she will be the liaison between you and your kids and/or your extended family. If this third of your life is miserable, then you will not be happy.

3. Find the best bed you can. You spend the final third of your life in bed either sleeping or, as my grandpa liked to say, "schtupping." Make sure the bed that you wake up in every morning has you feeling refreshed. Study your sleep habits to get the most out of yourself, like a finely tuned athlete.

All three of these keys to happiness start with you! I can't say it enough: *Surround yourself with the right people, and have meaningful relationships within your family.*

PICKING THE RIGHT PARTNER, ACCORDING TO MY FATHER: My father also had a simple set of rules for picking a business partner, and his rules could save anyone starting an organization from scratch. Rule 1, don't have a partner. A team doesn't need two head coaches. Rule 2, if you absolutely need a partner, find one who can finance your venture. Rule 3, if you're unable to find a partner as described in Rule 2, refer back to Rule 1.

EVALUATING THE BENEFITS OR DRAWBACKS OF YOUR FRIENDSHIPS

After family, the next most relative people in your life are your friends. Remember, you can choose your friends—that's the difference between the relativity of your family (which you're born into) and your compatriots. One of my biggest failures as a young person was that I wanted to be loved by everybody and wanted everyone to be my friend. Like a coach who is unable to get tough with his or her players and "cut" the bad apples, or a coach who doesn't have the guts to fire a subordinate coach or staff member who isn't pulling his or her weight, I was surrounding myself with the wrong people. I was limiting myself. I didn't have people around me who could teach me essential life lessons, and I paid the price for it.

After I became successful at a young age, I allowed everybody to drain me. That included my family—my parents, uncles, cousins—but most often, it was my so-called friends. I had no one around me to implement the balanced give-and-take of the **Ben Franklin effect**: I was helping everybody, but I wasn't asking for help at all.

> **BEN FRANKLIN EFFECT:** "He that has done you a kindness will be more ready to do you another, than he whom you yourself have obliged."
>
> —Ben Franklin

The Ben Franklin effect says that when others help you, you become an investment of theirs and you are more likely to receive help from them in the future. And if you aren't humble enough to ask for help, you will never get it. Because I was able to manifest millions of dollars, I lost my humility; I carried a belief that I didn't need anybody's advice or help. Through the mistakes I made during that time, I learned a great lesson: if friends turn their back on you, don't turn your back on them.

Live above the line with **accountability**: be compassionate and gracious. Do not live below the line in blame, shame, and justification. Be slow to anger with your team, abundant in love.

We mustn't act as if we deserved to be treated specially, nor must we separate ourselves as inferior or superior. We are all connected. When we have people in our life who don't bring the right energy to us or make us feel good, we must be aware of this and make the proper adjustments.

> **ACCOUNTABILITY:** The requirement to ask yourself two questions when situations arise: "What did I do to attract this to myself?" and, "What am I supposed to learn from this?" Then take the actions to learn from it and turn the lessons into new miracles.

The indicator that tells me if I am surrounding myself with the right friends is whether or not those friends make me feel good. If not, I let them fall away from me. I have too many other people connected to me in a positive way to waste my time with antagonists. I don't want to manifest negativity toward anyone, so I have to let those people go.

Shortly after my first financial windfall, everything began falling apart. I knew I had to call three specific friends who were very relative to me and cut the strings. I had known them my whole life. I called them and first asked for their forgiveness. I apologized, but I told them, "I can't be your friend anymore. I only pray for your happiness." I then stated, "This separation isn't about you. It's about me!"

I found it immensely difficult to summon the courage and explain that this change had nothing to do with them.

It was my problem. I added, "I'm sure for others, you're a wonderful person. But I can't find a way to like myself when I'm with you. I don't like the things I'm doing. I don't like the thoughts I am having. I can't engage in your flamboyant lifestyle anymore. I'm trying live as my higher self, and that cannot happen around you and your crowd." This may have been the hardest thing I had to do for my transformation, apart from telling my mother that I had lost everything in bankruptcy.

Maybe someday I'll be enlightened enough to figure out what it was about these three very close friends that made me feel and act this way, but every time we got together, we were doing the wrong things with the wrong people. It was not good that I was essentially retired at this point in my life because I ended up in seedy establishments in the middle of the day, surrounded by people who were not looking to support me, but to drain me.

I had to learn the hard way that if it bleeds, kill it, and if it grows, feed it. You see this happen in sports, when an organization's leaders fall in love with a player's talent and harm themselves by kowtowing to that athlete, to the detriment of the rest of their team. Josh Gordon, former Cleveland Brown, is a classic example. When he was able to stay on the field, Gordon possessed tantalizing skills, including posting 1,600+ yards and nine touchdowns in only 14 games in 2013. His off-the-field issues, however, served as a distraction, and I would argue that his influence on the team, even when he was suspended, was a major reason for the Browns' struggles in recent years. By staying committed to a player who was not committed to the organization, the Browns harmed the rest of the team's ability to succeed.

You don't always have to make decisions alone, which is why you should make sure you know your limitations. The Ben Franklin effect teaches us this: the best thing we can do is ask for help as well as offer help. When you can't do it all, take comfort in your friends, your "team." Be humble, and ask for help when you need it. Your team members have all types of gifts and abilities waiting to be discovered and put to good use for a higher purpose. That's how friends work best together.

You can choose to surround yourself with the right friends by considering the mutual capacities that you and each of your friends have and how this capacity can help both of you to achieve what you desire. Giving is easy. Even though we don't choose our families, most of us are willing to help them in times of need. And most of us are willing to help our friends, as well. So, we need to choose friends who can also help us. Surround yourself with those people who provide mutual benefits, not just those who are looking for a handout.

TESTING BUSINESS RELATIONSHIPS (AND YOURSELF)

Next, our business associates are less relative than our friends and even less relative than our family. We're born into our families, we can choose our friends, but our business associates are usually a combination of choice and fate. We respectively select some of our associates, and we also "inherit" some of them the way we inherit family members.

An interesting dynamic is created when we have this diverse combination of family and friends. Due to organizational hierarchy, there is always an inherent superiority or inferiority in a business, where people have to act and react to the actions of others who have more or less authority than themselves. This can also be true with family, but it is usually not the case with friends. Just as in a family setting, associates will test you just as children test their parents and prima donna athletes (constantly) test their coaches.

In business relationships, be prepared because everyone will test you, especially your team members. People naturally want to test boundaries and see what they can get away with. The best coaches don't demand respect from their team only at those times when they walk into the locker room. Instead, they have an expectation that their roster will live with a spirit of excellence. That expectation is something you need to drill into your squad, giving them the inspiration to push through the difficult times instead of simply looking for the easy way out. Share true stories, whether personal or observed, about former coworkers or employees who showed perseverance, or highlight current team members who display that attitude. As Lakers legend Jerry West said, "You can't get much done in life if you only work on the days when you feel good."[4]

Be clear in your expectations for those who might not be feeling their best, either mentally or physically. To keep your team aligned with organizational goals, give them positive reinforcement, tools, or strategies that are rooted in your core values. If you've got team members who are experiencing personal difficulties of some sort that are affecting their work, be empathetic. Encourage employees who seem a little stressed to take a walk and get some fresh air for a bit. Offer them a day or two off to clear their head. Do not let people habitually eschew their duties, however, because other team members will recognize this and try to test you in the same way.

Some associates will also test you in different fashions, such as looking to get the most money for doing the least amount of work. The best way to counter this is to require what I call an RIC for people who want a raise. Make them explain the *reasons* they deserve a pay increase, the *impacts* that they have on your team, and their *capabilities*, both the capabilities that they already have and the capabilities they need to keep working on. And no matter what, understand that when you find people who are conditioned to love what they do, they're the ones you want to surround yourself with.

Discovering those people is why at my company, Sports 1 Marketing, we've created such a robust intern program. It enables us to see who really loves doing what we do! That's the main reason why we don't pay our interns—not because we can't afford it but because we can see who truly wants to be here. Our interns are a highly diverse group of people. I have had everyone from 60-year-old men to NBA players and Olympians happily working for the experiences and opportunities that are provided by our business.

But, look, I get it. There is a reality to the intern situation: some people have student loans to pay back, some have parents on a strict budget, or they have parents who insist they get a job that pays a certain amount. What I say to all of those prospective interns who face that situation is, enjoy the challenge of successive events as they unfold. As long as you make a decision that is aligned with your values, there are no failures, just successes. Each of the things that we see as either challenges or failures, they are just successive events. Be aware of when you are acting in a certain manner that is not aligned with what you love to do, and make adjustments so that your lack of inspiration does not become a negative energy that you carry unconsciously.

It is important that you stay accountable for your own inspiration so that you are empowered to sacrifice more to get what you want (if you truly want it). You don't want to have to be constantly coached by others. Take accountability for yourself. Find what you love to do, and align it with what must be done. Sometimes, you do what you have to do until you get to a place where you can do what you love to do. But don't let your dream slip away in the process!

Change the way you look at things so the things you look at change. That's what you have to do with your circle of associates—your squad. Surround yourself with the right people. When I say "the right people," I mean the parts of the people you are most attracted to—the parts of others that bring you confidence, make you feel happy, or empower you to be your best self.

Have you ever met people who seemed to be pure evil? The only things they did were for themselves, they had nothing good to say, and they seemed to be in competition with ISIS for being truly bad? Or have you ever met someone you thought was terrific, and later something about him changed your mind, making you think he was a dick? I've had a couple people like those in my own life. Taking the right perspective on these feelings is absolutely essential for all leaders.

You also have to deal with others' opinions of you. You're never as good as they say you are, and you're never as bad. Don't believe your own press. And just because people are not nice to you doesn't mean they are not nice people or aren't nice to others.

Attract those people who will be nice to you even though they might not be nice to other people.

Some associates are constantly trying to show you how smart they are. Even more than asking questions, they love to answer them.

Most young associates want to be challenged, especially when they know their effort is going to be noticed and rewarded. They will give 110 percent if they are confident that there will be a beneficial outcome.

A team that has a collective belief of success will achieve it. They don't want false praise or accolades for just showing up. For example, I'm not a big fan of the participation trophies, like the ones in the commercial where the dad rips off the participant badge and writes "champs." Where is the empowerment in just showing up?

You have to know the difference between self-serving and righteous opinions. This is an important distinction, whether you're on the mentoring side, executive side, or management side of associates. Know the difference between self-serving anger and righteous anger. Even Jesus got angry, turning over tables of money in the temple. His motivation was just, his actions were focused, and his goal was to honor goodness. Righteous anger has purpose behind it, and it can be a motivator. Anyone who has watched a lot of football knows that some of the greatest coaches (Bill Parcells, Bill Belichick, Jim Mora, Don Shula, Vince Lombardi) have used righteous anger to unite their teams and goad them to victory.

Sometimes, you need to do something other than be angry to bring a team together. There was an experiment I conducted during one of my trainings: I told my employees not to think too much about the assignment, and then I instructed them, "I want you to get in your car, go to Home Depot, buy some wood, and make a pair of stilts." I gave them the money and told them to hurry.

What I wanted to see was whether or not they'd figure out the importance of teamwork. I wanted them to understand that if they wanted to build something great, they had to pick a leader, divide the work, and give specific tasks to people based on their particular skills. Instead, each of them went out and tried to do everything on his or her own, with lackluster results. This self-serving attitude led to undesirable outcomes for all, but it did a great job of instilling in the team the necessity of unity in accomplishing their goals.

Are you going to build an inferior set of stilts on your own? Or divide the work to get it done right?

We need to be accountable for our own actions even while we are all working together as one.

Anyone who has worked with me long enough knows that I'm a proponent of the tenet, "You must build your business so that it will continue to run in the absence of any one person in the leadership team." I need to know that my business still functions even if one of my top associates is missing. That's the way I built Sports 1 Marketing and S1Media, our award-winning media arm. Any key associate could leave tomorrow and the company, as a whole, would still succeed.

I've learned over the years that I need to "build the stilts" with more than one "carpenter," just as Nick Saban knows the necessity of having a fully stocked team roster, full of five-star recruits, to sustain a championship run. I need to know that if we're behind on sponsorship sales, I can grab the phone and in one day close the deals, or easily find someone else capable of doing so. I need to know that if somebody is not there to handle a specific project or task, there are six other people in line with the capabilities and know-how to fill in adequately. I need to know we have more than one car available for business trips. I need to know that I have two different bookkeepers who, in a pinch, can do each other's work.

With all of the little things I've learned, I try to empower others, which comes from these exercises that we do as a team in which we build situational knowledge and an awareness of how we succeed together. Our business will have plenty of revenue, even if none of the associates can build a fantastic pair of stilts by themselves.

> **CAN YOUR TEAM FUNCTION WITHOUT A QUARTER-BACK?** The 2017 Philadelphia Eagles showed that they could beat the best teams in the playoffs with a backup quarterback, ultimately making a successful Super Bowl run in February 2018 without their franchise quarterback, Carson Wentz.

LEARNING TO LEVERAGE EXPERIENCE

There are only two real values you have in business. The first is *relationship capital*, which is simply being kind to your future self, so that you are attracting to yourself or surrounding yourself with the right people with the right ideas. The other value is *situational knowledge*, which is the sum total of all the experiential knowledge you have acquired from your life, education, and relationships, as well as your mentors.

You're not going to get relationship capital by always telling other people what to do. Nor are you going to get situational knowledge by always telling people what to do. You need to go down to Home Depot, buy the wood, and attempt to learn to build the stilts yourself. You want to surround yourself with people who can either build good enough stilts to sustain themselves or find the resources to get it done. Assist them in building it, offer your help, and ask them to help you too.

I cannot overstate the value of having mentors. This starts with your having meaningful relationships with your family members, your friends, and your associates. I recommend maintaining a minimum of three mentor relationships at all times. These mentors are people you admire and want to emulate. If you want to be a great running back, punt returner, or kicker, then ask for advice from a great running back, punt returner, or kicker. If you want to be a great sports executive, seek the counsel of a great sports executive. If you surround yourself with what you want and the circumstances you want, the *law of attraction* will create what you want—rapidly and accurately.

This system of mentorship will expedite what you will become, improving your ability to make informed decisions. I wanted to learn how to become a billionaire, so I got luxury hotel developer Steve Wynn to be my mentor and help me understand his relationship with money (not his relationship with others), and how that perspective might work for me. I wanted to know how to be a speaker and write books, so I sought out help from the Napoleon Hill Foundation, since *Think and Grow Rich* is my favorite book, and got bestselling author Greg S. Reid to teach me how to do just that.

Last, I wanted to learn the *majesty of calmness* in pressure situations, so I asked former NFL quarterback Warren Moon to teach me how to attain it. Warren's guidance and coaching were invaluable when I was asked to throw out the first pitch at an Anaheim Angels game. Terrified, with a sold-out stadium on Sombrero Day (which actually set a Guinness World Record for the most people ever to wear sombreros at a baseball game), I utilized the majesty of calmness, which allowed me, with no pitching talent at all, to walk out onto a Major League Baseball field and remain calm and throw a knuckleball strike.

I wouldn't have been able to do that without Warren's having explained to me how it all works. I was able to leverage his experience. Warren, since the age of 18 years old, has often played in front of big crowds, occasionally approaching 100,000 people. He's always been known to keep his composure in tough situations. My favorite example came during an important game when he was quarterbacking the Minnesota Vikings. The Vikings were trailing with the clock winding down, but they had made their way into the red zone.

On a fourth-down play, Warren suddenly called a time-out, and his coach Denny Green began to freak out. When Warren came back to the sideline, Coach Green rattled off a list of things he thought that could have caused the time-out to be called. Did Warren see something with the defense that called for a different play? Was someone hurt or too tired to play? Was he hurt?

Warren, with a majesty of calmness, let his coach know what the issue was: he wanted some lip balm. Coach Green freaked out again, yelling for staffers to get his quarterback some lip balm. And what did Warren do? He used the lip balm he was given, said thank you, walked back onto the field, and ran the same play they had called before the time-out, throwing a touchdown to take the lead.

Knowing the countless experiences like this that Warren had gone through, I asked him, "When you came out of the tunnel, you had to be nervous. What did you do?" His answer gave me the confidence to succeed. How long do you think it would have taken someone like me to learn what Warren already knew from his own experiences? Finding the composure to deal with the thousands of people cheering me on (or booing me) while I took the field would have been nearly impossible. But I was blessed to have had his mentorship and help, which saved me lots of effort and provided me with insights that would have been tough to acquire otherwise.

Everyone can find great mentors. The first thing you need to do is to be more interested than interesting. Define the reasons you need a mentor, the impact that mentor is going to have on your life, and the ability of that mentor to guide you in your quest for what you want. What kind of coach do you need? Then, look into the best way to find that person, and most importantly, *ask him or her to be your mentor*. As you know, you don't get unless you ask.

We are curious people. Use your inquisitive nature as a way to connect with your mentors—as a conduit for helping them help you discover the truth, whatever that may be for you. Why do we want to discover the truth? Because the truth vibrates the fastest. Truth vibrates at a speed where past, present, and future are all one. When we vibrate at the speed of truth, we are extremely happy.

A great way to encourage your associates and mentees to find their truth is without words. Use a nod or handshake or a smile, even a silly thumbs-up. Be ready (and consistent) with praise, suggestions, personal perspective, and honest critique when they ask, "What do you think?"

An associate's encouragement takes away the fear of failure. This will confirm that you have nothing to lose, as long as you are living with gratitude, empathy, accountability, and effective communication. A boss's encouragement takes away the fears that victory isn't sufficient, confirming for the team that the team's members have everything to win instead of having everything to lose, proving that if you change the way you look at things, the things you look at change.

Clarity, balance, and focus bring confidence, whether you are a leader or an associate. Hence, why both of these statements are valid: Is an associate helping you get clarity, balance, and focus so you can be confident that you have nothing to lose? Or is a boss giving you clarity, balance, and focus so you can be confident that you have everything to win? It's all your own perspective.

POSTGAME WRAP-UP

When you surround yourself with the right people, it's not about anyone else. It's about you! I know this is counterintuitive, but there is only one person who is accountable for positioning himself or herself to build a team in the first place, and that is you. Herein lies the answer to almost every problem that people will confront you with in life—today, tomorrow, and throughout time.

Commonly, people believe that they are sustained by everything but themselves. That's the biggest problem I see. Some people think they're sustained by their parents, their money, the sun, by food—everything but themselves. Some people place their faith in the most trivial and insane symbols like money, expensive clothing, influence, and prestige—endless forms of nothingness that are endowed with magical powers. All these things are inadequate replacements for truth and love in yourself.

Learn to love you. If you love yourself, you'll attract the right roster of people to take the field with, whether it's the right people among your family members, friends, associates, or mentors. To love, you also need to be thankful and forgiving, communicate effectively, and be accountable. It's all within you. I can give you the ideas, I can give you righteous anger, and I can inspire you, but you have to believe in *the power of you* to empower others to believe in themselves. When you take the proper perspective, when you are grateful and empathetic to others, you will improve your decision-making acumen and change the perspectives of people who surround you.

Before leaders can build the strongest of teams, they need the inner strength to deal with the challenges ahead. Coaches who are strong and steadfast in their values are better prepared to build relationships with family members, friends, associates, and recruits, and they are equally well prepared to make the decision to end relationships. Strong values attract a strong team, a team that can be coached to react to any situation put before them. But it takes a capable and inspiring leader to make it all come together for victory.

A self-assured leader has the confidence to ask for help when needed, identifying those with situational knowledge who can provide advice and being humble enough to seek it out. These are the keys to building a winning roster.

2

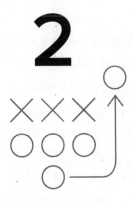

Offensive/ Defensive Mindset

PREGAME ANALYSIS

Once you have surrounded yourself with the right team, you must create a game plan with the right mindset. Having a negative mindset is one of the biggest mistakes that anyone can make, so you need to arm yourself to defend against any negativity that comes your way. Make sure your defense is ready for any offense. How do you accomplish this? You must first understand how your mind works—consciously, subconsciously, and unconsciously. Just like the three phases of football (offense, defense, and special teams), you need to be successful in all three areas in order to consistently win.

That success comes from controlling the inputs that go into our mind, focusing on the positive and overcoming the negative. It is our strong core values that empower us and provide the inspiration to push forward toward progress, even when we are mired in a slump. Speaking of value, a cornerstone of the optimal mindset comes from a drive to provide value to others, a quality that has helped to build the most prosperous careers in sports and business.

A leader's mindset is derived from his or her thought processes, whether that comes from his or her conscious, subconscious, or unconscious mind. It is for precisely that reason that we must be aware of our recurring thought patterns, as well as the new ideas and information that we take in. We need to learn to manage our negative thoughts, or those that are not adding value to our pursuits, in order to avoid repeating the same mistakes or to shed a victim mentality. There are all sorts of pressures that we experience (or create for ourselves) when we are making a tough call, but with the right mindset, we can avoid common pitfalls, such as negative self-talk or decision fatigue. With the right roster of thoughts and well-balanced personal values, we will be empowered as leaders to overcome slumps or obstacles, and we'll learn to avoid manifesting the same mental struggles over and over.

We start with the decision-making mindset. There are three minds with which we make our decisions: the conscious, subconscious, or unconscious minds. Our *conscious mind* evaluates what people think, what people say, and what people do. And it takes time to get the conscious alignment necessary to make a decision. Looking at what people think, say, and do helps us evaluate how aligned others are with our *foundational values*: our *personal values* (such as health, character, and love), *experiential values* (the "dummy tax" I've paid, and my situational knowledge), *giving values* (how I'm going to help humanity), and *receiving values* (how much we are going to make or what we are going to receive). At certain times of our life, we put a different emphasis on those values, so there is not an equal balance of 25 percent personal values, 25 percent experiential values, 25 percent giving values, and 25 percent receiving values.

We have to know the balance of the values that we're looking at. Sometimes, a decision is made 100 percent on our personal values. Sometimes it's made 100 percent on our giving values, and so on. So, we have to keep that in context with our conscious decision making, and we have to know how the actions of others are aligned with our core values.

Then, we must realize that there's another level of analysis that must be done for our subconscious. The *subconscious mind* deals with the countless things that we believe. We assess the actions and intentions of others and whether those are aligned with our values and beliefs. Belief becomes aligned with the entire roster of our thoughts, both conscious and subconscious.

The reason for this is that what we believe vibrates faster than our conscious thought. Our subconscious vibrates faster than our conscious. So, when we make a snap decision or call an audible, we rely on our beliefs, based on our whole life's experiences. The totality of our personal values, experiential values, giving values, and receiving values are input into our subconscious and our unconscious. It is our *unconscious competency*, the energy that we carry, that attracts to us what we have in our life.

MAKE SURE YOUR MIND RUNS THE RIGHT PATTERNS

Our unconscious competency is responsible for all of the patterns that we have in our decisions and actions. No matter what we think, say, and do, what our values are today, or what we believe, there are certain problems that keep coming into our life—repeating patterns of the same objections, the same obstacles, the same voids, the same unbeneficial or problematic relationships. Of course, there is also the same "good stuff" that we receive repeatedly, as a result of what we attract subconsciously or unconsciously. We can have a competency that we are unaware of and that allows us to be doing, thinking, saying, and believing all the right things, but still we might not be attracting what we want. So, how do we control all of these conscious, subconscious, and unconscious inputs to help make a decision?

There was a paper written in 1973 by a researcher named Paul Slovic that described a study in which researchers took horse handicappers and allowed them to choose 5 out of 88 basic pieces of information for them to use to pick winning horses.[1] The study looked at all of these different handicappers' betting patterns, and what horses they gambled on, as well as how many bets they placed, and how often these bets were successful. What the researchers found was that decision making based on those five pieces of information resulted in the handicappers being right 17 percent of the time.

The researchers then gave the handicappers additional information, upping the variables they could choose to 10. Now the handicappers learned more of what others thought, said, or did regarding each horse. This altered their subconscious belief: the handicappers felt that because they had more information, they were more likely to be right. But once again, when they tallied up all the bets, even with the additional information, the handicappers were still hovering around 17 percent success rates.

The gamblers were then presented with even more inside information: 20 and 40 different variables' worth, some of the best "inside information" that a handicapper could hope for. And what changed? Only the handicappers' belief that they would be more accurate—that's all. Once again, their unconscious competency was accurate only 17 percent of the time.

What's the lesson we can learn from this study? We waste a great deal of time not understanding the effects of the information that we consciously and subconsciously take in and how that influences the unconscious energy that we carry. Our unconscious is what guides our in-the-moment decision making, and this is why it is necessary to understand how information, good and bad, manifests itself in the results of those split-second choices.

UNCONSCIOUS COMPETENCY

Take a look at the decisions you've made in the past that led to outcomes attracting what you didn't want. Try to see the repetitive thought patterns that you acted upon when faced with similar decisions. We all make wrong decisions sometimes, but through careful analysis of the repetitive choices we make with our gut, we can raise our awareness and reduce these patterns of missteps going forward. Think of this analysis as being like film study in sports, where you are looking at the mistakes you make each week so that you can make adjustments to prevent those same gaps in your thinking or actions going forward.

Have you ever heard of a basketball player who is on a hot shooting streak referred to as being "unconscious"? There is a reason for that. When we do something over and over, the action gets ingrained in our cellular memory, which is something you can take advantage of so that you can be more efficient, effective, and statistically successful. This rapid thinking (and execution) is why you must program your mind the way athletes program their muscles. You don't want to program your mind to do the wrong things. You want to find your decision-making "stroke" and find a groove that you can stay in.

UNCONSCIOUS COMPETENCY: A task, ability, or decision you are able to execute successfully without thinking, like breathing.

If we're not getting what we want out of our choices, then we need to make a change. Now, how do we effectuate that change? We change it with a consistent (meaning every day) and persistent (meaning without quitting) enjoyment of the pursuit of the truth or our potential. Be inspired to chase your higher self when it comes to awareness and decision making. In a pragmatic way, that means that we have to control our conscious mind first. Our conscious mind tells the body what to think, say, and do. The body has a memory. The body's memory is in our cells. Every cell has its own memory. Our subconscious mind can be controlled by what we feed it because it's going to remember. We need to feed our subconscious "good stuff" every day. We don't want to feed it the "bad stuff." What does it mean to feed our subconscious the "good stuff"? We start by thinking about positive things. What are those positive things? The things we truly want. Our desires, whatever we believe will make us happy and fulfilled. If we're thinking about something that we *don't* want, all we're going to get is more of what we don't want.

We need to cancel these negative thoughts when they creep into our conscious, to prevent them from becoming a subconscious belief. I believe when we think of something that we don't want, it is imperative to say or think "Cancel."

Tell our body straight out that we don't want that negativity in our cellular memory because from there, it will eventually become our unconscious competency.

We've all had thoughts that keep us up at night, despite our desire to let them go, and sometimes we can't help what we think, due to the patterns of our conscious will. Certain things keep coming back to us in thoughts, whether they are in words or impulsive actions. We need to understand that these repetitive thoughts are what our belief system is attracting to us. We've already mentioned how important our "roster of thoughts" is. Just as there is with any team roster, there tends to be lots of consistency from day to day, week to week, and month to month. Most of this roster stays relatively unchanged, which is why it is essential to ensure that our thoughts—our positivity—is adding value to our decision-making process.

We can control this vast number of thoughts with the countless information inputs that we have each day, focusing on the "good stuff," which prepares us for what might occur in the future and inspires us to raise our awareness. Doing this consistently shifts the repetitive subconscious thoughts that make up our unconscious beliefs, the convictions that we aren't entirely aware of. The things that sit in our subconscious have to be cleaned out on a continual basis, which is accomplished by clearing our mind.

That's the main reason why I use meditation to assist in my decision making when I'm faced with a tough call. Instead of taking action by thinking, saying, and doing, I simply go back to center, find a moment of peace, and clear my mind. Decisions become clearer, more effective, more efficient, and more successful once we are in a calm, meditative state. Getting to this state is not too difficult to accomplish once you have established a baseline. You don't even have to know how to meditate to attain this calm state. Sit up straight. Breathe in through your nose and out through your mouth six times, what I call the "Six Breaths of Buddha." Simply do it consistently, every single day, to shift your energy and make better decisions.

BOX OUT NEGATIVE SELF-TALK AND PRESSURE

Negative self-talk is something that we all deal with, and it hampers our confidence and ability to succeed, often without us realizing it. Positive thoughts and actions bring more positivity, which is why it is important for us to focus on training our brains to be positive. A lack of confidence can hurt anyone's chances for success, but this is especially true for athletes and executives alike. One of my favorite ways to avoid negative thinking and instill subconscious and unconscious confidence is through positive repetition. For athletes, having these positive mantras can help affirm their confidence in their abilities, preparing their mind to work in unison with their body.

One of the best examples of this is a set of mantras called "The Athlete's Litany." This set of phrases is meant to be repeated every day, until they are a subconscious belief and eventually an unconscious competency. These can be easily adapted and incorporated into the routine of any leader, imbuing confidence in the approach he or she is taking to solving a problem. Creating a Leader's Litany of your own can help give you more resolve in your actions, leading to better performance and a mindset capable of handling any challenging decision that may come your way:

The Leader's Litany

- I have passion for my job.
- I am committed to the enjoyment of the pursuit of my potential.
- I will provide as much value as I can and *ask big* in return.
- I will give 100 percent of my focus and intention to excelling in my role at work and helping others to do the same.
- If I focus on progress and not perfection, I will succeed.
- I will think and talk positively.
- I will get out of my comfort zone and into the learning zone.
- I will not let my ego get in the way.
- I will be of service.

Often, when we get into a position to make decisions, there's a certain amount of tension that occurs due to our negative perceptions or a lack of confidence in ourselves. Game shows on TV are fantastic at creating situations rife with tension. They create physical, conscious conditions to make sure contestants feel the pressure, almost as if they're being interrogated. Time is a great way to put artificial pressure on decisions, and you must pay attention to how time is influencing your choices. A time crunch makes just about everybody feel the pressure to act. Many a time has there been a two-minute drill in football where the team with the ball cracks under pressure, turning it over and losing the game. So, what's the best thing to do when you are put under pressure? Go back to center. Don't react. Just find a sense of calmness, and the right decision will come to you.

Occasionally, you will run into something called *decision fatigue* that can devastate your ability to make quick, accurate decisions. This occurs when you're repeatedly trying to force an outcome instead of allowing things to happen. You're constantly worried and making decision after decision, week after week, season after season. You're either taking too long to decide or you're basing your decisions on the wrong facts, or you're overanalyzing the situation and getting in your own way. Again, this can be combatted by finding peace, going back to center, and making a call based on your newly elevated awareness.

AVOID NEGATIVE REPETITION WITH TRUTHS

Every once in a while, something happens in our life that keeps coming back to confront us, even after our attempts to get rid of it. This is due to the fact that there are certain things that trigger the emotions that lie within our unconscious competency. If we cannot shift the energy from these issues, they will manifest themselves and skew our decision-making process. If we have certain unconscious competencies that are not positive, one way to cure our unconscious competency is through the Four Great Truths: *gratitude*, *empathy*, *accountability*, and *effective communication*.

The first way to help ourselves if we are unable to cancel and clear our energy is to simply be grateful for whatever is causing us issues. Gratitude is a perspective that can turn something bad that's happened (or is happening) to us into something we can appreciate. This means that we are thankful for the times we get "sacked" or strike out and that, much like the financial definition of the word *appreciate*, we realize these difficulties add value to us, as situational knowledge to leverage for future decisions.

Gratitude is *res ipsa loquitur*, or "that which speaks for itself" in English. It's a truth. It's a potential that everyone has inside them—to think, say, do, and believe the right things in order to be grateful for even the most negative things that sit within their own unconscious competencies. We can also affect our unconscious competency with forgiveness, for ourselves and for others. We need to forgive ourselves for whatever we experience because if we are unable to forgive ourselves for mistakes and bad decisions, we will also be unable to forgive others for theirs. Take errors in baseball, for example. Over time, even the best defenders will make dozens or hundreds of errors. In fact, 8 out of the top 20 leaders in career errors are in the Hall of Fame.

> **ERROR:** An error in judgment is an opportunity for improvement, as long as you are accountable for your mistake.

This is a clear connection to the next value that empowers us to shift our subconscious belief: accountability. Accountability means accepting responsibility for making the wrong decisions, taking them as an opportunity to analyze our missteps and what we did subconsciously (and unconsciously) to attract those mistakes in judgment. Then, we must make a conscious decision to not only take corrective action but also to make the most of the learning opportunity that has been provided and to leverage our newfound situational knowledge in future determinations. When we combine gratitude for the incidents that have happened, forgive ourselves for what has happened, and take accountability, we can then use this opportunity as a chance to help other people to learn from our own experiences.

Effective communication comes next, which entails sharing our knowledge and experiences with others, which can shift our own perspective and our own energy, knowing it is a gift to provide gratitude, forgiveness, and accountability to others. A coach who knows what to do to win but can't get his or her strategy across will never be an effective coach. You can't just *know* how to win; you must be able to teach others in order to bring your vision to reality. Faith is also an important factor when choosing a path to take, and it works two ways, in both good and bad decision making. People think of faith only in good decision making, but sometimes we have faith in what we don't have and end up attracting more of what we don't have.

Sharing a plan effectively is immensely easier if we have faith in that plan. If we continue to make bad decisions, whether it's consciously or with an unconscious energy that we're carrying, we will fall into a pattern that is difficult to get out of. Just as a hitter occasionally falls into a slump, we cannot make this state our norm.

A typical *slump* has four stages: *prosperity, recession, depression,* and *recovery.* We must push through the tough stages to get to the good. A winning streak always follows a losing streak, so know that we're not a victim of whatever our current circumstances are. It's just our story and our journey.

> **SLUMP:** A prolonged experience of negative outcomes, often changed by hard work, focus, and renewed inspiration. Blue Jay and Dodger great Shawn Green has often cited his month-long slump during the 1997 season, which resulted in his benching, as a turning point in his career.

We're not victims of missteps and manipulations, interceptions or fumbles. They are just things that happen—that happen to everyone. And they are an opportunity for us to be grateful. An opportunity for us to forgive ourselves. An opportunity for us to be accountable and a chance for us to motivate others and live inspired lives.

Imagine what a caterpillar feels like, crawling around until suddenly one day everything changes. He ends up hung upside down in the dark. Imagine what that caterpillar feels like: he is walking on this beautiful grass, and all of a sudden, he is literally hanging upside down in the dark. Sounds like what happens when you are faced with a tough decision? Sounds like a tough, tough place to be . . . hanging upside down in the dark, with no gratitude, forgiveness, accountability, or effective communication. Just the pressure to fight and struggle from the dark into the light.

What does the caterpillar do? He doesn't quit. He tries to knock himself out of the cocoon he put himself into. He works to find a solution to the problem, right? Tired of hanging upside down in the dark, he works with all his might to figure out a different way to get out of that cocoon. The caterpillar keeps working, exploring, figuring things out, until he's eventually strong enough to break through. Instead of walking on the grass like he did before, he flies and becomes one of the most beautiful creatures on earth. And he is completely free, manifesting what he desires.

Most people have had challenges when they have felt almost like they were hanging upside down, at least for a day or two, in the dark. We need to make the decision to be grateful for those experiences from beginning to end, to be accountable and more motivated every day. Sometimes we're in a cocoon longer than other people, or it's darker and colder than it is for others. It doesn't matter. We have the power to get out. The Universe is not going to give us anything we can't break out of. It may test our patience, but that's where true greatness comes from. It comes from the ability to consistently, persistently enjoy the pursuit of our potential.

No matter how deep a slump we get into, we have to have a mindset that's based on gratitude, empathy, accountability, and effective communication, and we have to understand that our mindset has three different realms of thought: the conscious mind, the subconscious mind of beliefs, and the unconscious competency that's developed with those same four values.

If we live inspired, we can inspire others, which also allows us to be more aware and make better decisions at the same time. Heightened awareness means we know simple things, like whether to go left or right, whether to go to a party or not, or whether to buy or sell. When to swing at a pitch or when to let it go by. It also serves us well when dealing with more complicated matters, like what to ask for in a business agreement. There are a million different decisions, simple and complex, that need to be made in a timely fashion, so we're not fatigued about making decisions and we can be our best selves.

A MINDSET TO PROVIDE MORE VALUE

There are three mindsets that help us make the best decision, by raising our awareness and shifting our energy, so that we live a life of abundance. If we make decisions based on having enough, we're going to end up with not enough. And if we decide based on just having enough, we're going to have just enough. And, if we decide from a place of more than enough . . . *you guessed it:* there's enough of everything for everyone including us. This belief in abundance is an energy, and that's truly where the 100/20 Rule comes from, being of service.

The 100/20 Rule is simple: believe that you are giving $100 worth of value and asking for $20 in return. Carry that energy as if your job were to consistently provide exponentially more value than what you are asking for in return.

The people who make the biggest difference in any organization are those who know the value that they bring to the field (or negotiating table). In a land of scarcity, contracts, and salary caps, there are individuals who are able to provide much more value than they ask for in return, and they end up changing an organization's destiny.

One of my favorite stories comes from Eagles General Manager Howie Roseman, a former unpaid intern turned GM and owner of a Super Bowl ring. Howie actually began his journey to the front office as a young child. As a first grader flying to Florida, young Howie was serendipitously seated next to Jack Elway, who at the time was the head coach for San Jose State. The two connected over Howie's Yankees hat because Jack's son, a guy by the name of John Elway, had been drafted by the Bronx Bombers.

The two talked football for hours, which left young Howie believing that his dream of working for an NFL team was possible and holding Elway's business card in his pocket. Emboldened by his experience and his passion for the game, he also showed persistence in chasing his dream: Howie sent an estimated 1,100 letters to NFL teams throughout high school, college, and law school, before landing an internship with the Eagles.

NFL front-office vets, like my buddies Mike Tannen-baum and Joe Banner, in describing how far Howie went to get an interview, have said that Howie was one of the most persistent people they have ever met. Indeed, Howie has joked that he was a bit of a "stalker." He even went to law school with the goal of specializing in salary caps and nego-tiation, in order to set himself apart from other front-office candidates in the NFL's new salary cap era.

Once he landed an internship, Howie involved himself in the team's scouting process, gaining invaluable situational knowledge about how to identify, evaluate, and determine the value of physical talent. He even helped the staff research contracts, adding even more critical situational knowledge for future use by quantifying the monetary value of team members. Howie provided the Philadelphia Eagles organiza-tion with as much value as he could, which is why he quickly moved up the ranks, trusting that he would be rewarded with value in return. This strategy worked, as he eventually became the youngest general manager in NFL history at 34 years old (although that record has since been broken), and he had his big breakthrough with a Super Bowl Championship in 2018.

This strategy is one to cling to when we're in trouble, when we're down, when we feel challenged, when we've lost everything: serve our way out of it. Be of service and provide value.

One of the best examples of a player who understands the importance of being selfless and serving others can be seen in NBA superstar Kevin Durant. When he first signed with the Golden State Warriors, he had a singular focus: championships. After losing to my favorite team, the Cleveland Cavaliers, in the NBA Finals during his first season as a Warrior, Durant became more focused on acquiring rings than ever. He declined a $27 million player option and took a pay cut of almost $10 million in order to save the Warriors some money and keep the team together, in a similar move to what the Miami Heat's Big 3 of LeBron James, Dwyane Wade, and Chris Bosh did in forming their "super team" several years earlier.

That pay cut enabled the Warriors to keep important players like Andre Iguodala and Shaun Livingston on their roster, which ultimately led to the team winning back-to-back NBA Championships. Not only that, Durant's ventures outside of basketball, such as his media company, have thrived with his additional exposure as a star player in one of the best markets in the country. Later on, he was able to re-sign with the Warriors at a value much closer to what he's worth, with his most recent contract paying him over $30.5 million for the 2018 to 2019 season.

Durant also knows the branding benefits of multiple championship rings and MVP trophies, which he has in large part due to his selfless actions and his trust that things will work out when he provides as much value as possible and asks big.

Life—and business—is simple to me because I know one thing: the 100/20 Rule. If I give more than I ask for, nobody will say no. Everyone will trade my $100 bill for their $20. This comes from an energy, the inspiration to tell people we want to provide this and then ask for something back of lesser value. Can we believe it and feel it? It doesn't matter what we tell others—they have to be able to not only listen to what we think, say, and do, not only believe it, but feel it unconsciously. There can be no doubt in their mind. There is no decision to make. It's just the natural course of energy.

Once we give our value to somebody else and we are of service, we have been released. I'll tell you what that means. We tend to put conditions or judgments on people that we give things to. We often don't give unconditionally. We give with expectations. Instead, we need to take the position that once we give to others, we've been released. Once we've given, it does not matter what we have previously said, thought, done, or believed. We have done our deed, and we are accountable for that deed, but not its results for others. Just as if we picked up a piece of trash, returned a shopping cart to the corral, held a door for somebody, picked up a teammate (or opponent) off the ground, or helped an old lady across the street, if we give unconditionally, regardless of what our motivation is, we've done our job.

Give unconditionally, in good faith, regardless of what others think, say, or do and regardless of whether any manipulation has occurred. Once we've given, once we've agreed, we're released by our good deed. Whether we were motivated to act by our conscious, subconscious, or unconscious mind, our decision making speaks for itself, *res ipsa loquitir.*

POSTGAME WRAP-UP

In summary, there is a mindset to making effective decisions dictated by the three interconnected minds that affect our thoughts, actions, and energy: the conscious mind, composed of what we think, say, and do; the subconscious mind, built from what we believe; and the unconscious mind, formed by our unconscious competency, or what we naturally attract with the energy we carry. Clear your mind and control the input into your roster of thoughts, so that only healthy subconscious thoughts exist.

You want a roster filled with ideas and principles that puts you in a position for success—that is, a roster that does not undermine your ability to act decisively and appropriately when an unexpected situation pops up. Doing this evaluation every day will help you to attract subconsciously more positive things that you want in your life, be they people, actions, or thoughts.

This evaluation of conscious information intake and subconscious thought will then affect your natural energy, your DNA, your code, your unconscious competency. You will walk around like a human magnet, attracting everything that you desire. You'll be like those players who always finds themselves around the ball.

Allow things to happen by getting out of your own way, with the values of gratitude, empathy, accountability, and effective communication. This will not only keep you inspired, but it will also allow you to inspire and elevate others, to elevate yourself and carry an unconscious energy of serving others.

Always be energetically giving a $100 bill and receiving only a $20 bill in return. In this way, you will allow things to happen and allow others to liberate themselves because they won't be able to see any reason to not provide value to others.

We can be grateful for opportunities to give and be accountable, and we can communicate effectively the value that we bring as well as the value we want from the Universe in return. That's how we make decisions with the correct mindset. Making that decision in the right mindset will lead to us manifesting what we desire.

3

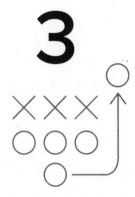

Coaching Trees and Growth

PREGAME ANALYSIS

Nothing accelerates a leader's growth and knowledge base better than finding individuals who sit in a position that the leader desires to be in and tapping into their experiences. Identifying the right mentors, based on their situational knowledge and core values, is easier said than done, but the challenge of creating a relentless learning environment is one you must take if you want to put yourself in the best possible position to succeed. Coaches can not only help you make the right decisions at the right time but they can also save you from making the same kinds of mistakes they have made in their own leadership roles, and from paying the same prices for those mistakes.

An understanding of how to create a mentorship tree, not only for yourself but for your other team members, is key for any organization because this additional guidance fosters the personal and professional development that creates sustainable value throughout the organization. Being coached by the right individuals is often as simple as allowing yourself to be humble enough to ask those you respect for help and being respectful of the value that they are providing you. If you can impart these beliefs to your team, you will empower them to push past any fear of failure and create a system of mentorship that drives your team to countless victories.

THE IMPORTANCE OF A MENTORING TREE

Mentoring and coaching are two of the best ways to improve your decision-making acuity. You look at everything that you do through a lens that is relative, whether it's personal or professional. Looking through a lens of productivity and accessibility will allow you to constantly expand and accelerate your vibration and productivity, which will in turn create more action and more value. Accessibility works two ways:

how accessible you are to others and how quickly you can access what you want. That lens forces you to create more efficiency in your decision making, which creates more productivity.

Successful organizations are set up such that even if you're a coach or a mentor, you are always a mentee as well. This enables you to leverage two things that make a company successful: relationship capital and situational knowledge. You have relationship capital if you utilize the ask and the attract methodology (asking in person or attracting in person, via the phone, email, or social media). If you and your team members are all capable of doing that, your relationship capital will expand—and at the same time, you will also leverage your team's collective situational knowledge.

The efficiency and productivity of your decisions will rise exponentially if you are focused on leveraging situational knowledge. This can be accomplished in two ways. One is to give help. "Hey, this is how you should do it. I've been here before. Here are the mistakes that I made." The second way is through accessing your relationship capital. People need the relationship capital in place that can assist them with identifying the right production system, the best method of quality control, and so on. Some people are unable to ask for help, or they don't have the right mentorship in place for their unique roles, which can create difficulties. To avoid these types of issues and target applicable mentors, my company created a model that asks, "What do you want to learn, and whom do you want to learn it from?"

BEING HUMBLE ENOUGH
TO ASK FOR HELP

Identify those people who have the right situational knowledge or experience or who sit in a position that you want to be in. To do that, you have to be one thing: radically humble. Realize that most people love to give. Most people freely give their advice to those that value it. Most people love to share their experience, their situational knowledge. Even their relationship capital—most people love to give to those they emotionally connect with. The reason they love to give is ego based. It's really not a humble thing at all. They feel separate or superior when they're giving, and in a scarce world, they feel better about themselves when they give. You can always identify humble people because not only can they give unconditionally (without expectation or trading) but they can also ask for help.

When it comes to humility, I like to talk about how the practice of humility opens your world to new skills and knowledge, key components for people who strive for greatness in their decision making. Take Kobe Bryant, for example. Most know him as one of the best scorers in NBA history, a champion by any definition of the word. But Bryant did not let his previous successes cloud his judgment when starting the media portion of his career. He was humble enough to call upon others who had different skill sets and a different knowledge base, and that's why his early forays into media, such as his Oscar Award–winning short film *Dear Basketball,* have been such a hit with audiences.

In an interview with Jimmy Fallon on *The Tonight Show,* Bryant shared the simple, humble way that he was able to attach such respected names as composer John Williams and animator Glen Keane to his project: he asked. As Bryant told the audience, when it comes to learning any skill or gaining knowledge when you are unsure, "the best way to learn is to reach out and ask."[1] Even one of sports' all-time greats understands that the practice of humility will help leaders avoid the traps that their egos are apt to send them into.

There are so many things that today's successful executives are not asking for help with because of their ego or lack of humility. Things change really fast, both in the sports world and in business. So many professionals are losing by not using Snapchat, Instagram, Facebook, or LinkedIn, simply because they are not humble enough to ask. I was business coaching an executive of a very large company, and I said, "Oh, are you using LinkedIn?"

"No."

"Are you using Snapchat?"

"No."

"Instagram?"

"No."

"Why not?"

"Oh, I can't figure that out."

I said, "Excuse me, you went to Harvard undergrad, Wharton Business School, you have an MBA and a PhD from Columbia, and you're telling me that my five-year-old can figure out Instagram and you can't? I have employees who have taught themselves to speak English that can figure out LinkedIn—*and you can't?* You write books on economics. You're in the *Wall Street Journal* analyzing complex business situations—*and you can't?*"

> **HUMILITY:** A state of being in which you are able to admit that you don't know what you don't know and you are willing to ask others for help.

What is that person's problem? Is it education, experience, or knowledge? No. It's simple humility. This holds true for CEOs and their business just as it does for NBA All-Stars and NFL football teams. There are owners of football teams and business executives who simply refuse to ask for help. They want to be the head coach, general manager, and the quarterback, all at once. We've seen them throughout the years. We saw a trend where the best head coaches, all of a sudden, wanted to be the general manager as well, with some even wanting to be a partial owner. There are well-known owners who are always intermingling in as many aspects of the organization as possible, exerting their control.

It doesn't work that way in an efficient company. We have to give and receive help. We do that through the four values: *gratitude, empathy, accountability,* and *effective communication,* very simple things that are at the core of being a mentor. Humility goes along with gratitude. Humility goes along with forgiveness. Humility goes along with accountability and the ability to communicate effectively.

CHOOSING MENTORS AND ALIGNING WITH THEIR VALUES

Utilize the ability to understand whom you want as a mentor and whom you want to (or need to) mentor and why. Communicate those goals effectively to your mentors and mentees. Let them know your expectations. I've had people come to me and ask for mentorship because they want to be a great quarterback and they know I've worked with tons of great quarterbacks.

I say, "Well, let me give you the first piece of advice. Go to my business partner, Warren Moon. He would be a much better choice to mentor you on how to be a great quarterback. If you want to be a sports agent, start a business, get funding, grow or scale a business, write a book, speak to audiences, or be a business coach, I can help you because I have situational knowledge for you to leverage in all of those areas. I don't know how to make you a great quarterback, but I know how to find one."

People often have tons of situational knowledge that they can teach you, but you need to be careful whom you ask because there are always things that people don't know.

In fact, in the world of sports, one of the things you rarely hear is, "I don't know." Egos play a huge part when athletes are interviewed. Many times, they go below the line in blame, shame, justification, and or some other ego-based avoidance. Very rarely do you see an athlete who makes a mistake that costs the game say, "Yeah, I'm accountable."

John Wooden, like most great coaches and executives,

always took accountability. And his famous Pyramid of Success could be seen as a mentoring tree. I was blessed enough to witness its impactful message firsthand . . . at Stanford, of all places. Warren and I got to walk onto the field on Stanford superstar Andrew Luck's senior day, due to our relationship with quarterback guru George Whitfield.

Before we headed to the field, we were sitting in Stanford's cafeteria, and right there on the wall was a giant poster of John Wooden's pyramid. UCLA's greatest coach (and maybe the NCAA's greatest coach of all time) sits in Stanford's cafeteria, his name emblazoned along with his Pyramid of Success. This is a story of mentorship winning out over ego. Stanford won the 2017–18 Capital One Cup Championship, achieving something no school had done before, winning for the achievements of both its men's and women's sports programs. This is in large part because they were humble enough to take the opportunity to learn from their biggest rival's best coach of all time. Not only that, but the poster was put up in the cafeteria for everyone to see, not just the athletes. That's humility. That's mentorship.

Why would they put it up there? Because that Pyramid of Success is like *gratitude*, *empathy*, *accountability*, and *effective communication*. It is a foundation for everyone to align with, take action with, and make adjustments with. It empowers everyone to take positive action.

Before I began to focus on empowering and mentoring people, I had always thought there was a distinction: kids who had grown up poor or had experienced being broke were more *empowered* than kids who had grown up with financial stability and who felt *entitled*. Then, I started an internship program where I learned a valuable lesson. It turned out that almost 50 percent of my interns came to us through referrals. What I discovered was that the ratio of empowered to entitled interns was always equal between the two groups, and it didn't matter if they had grown up rich or poor.

A person's upbringing doesn't make him or her empowered or entitled. I've seen totally broke people who were entitled, not living in gratitude, empathy, accountability, and effective communication. I have also met extremely wealthy kids who went to private schools and had every advantage in the entire world who were among the most empowered people I have ever met.

The only difference between empowered and entitled is that the people who live with strong core values are empowered. Gratitude gives them perspective, no matter what they have or lack. Empathy gives them forgiveness, no matter what they've done. Accountability gives them the power to move forward. Effective communication gives them the power to connect with others, help them, and ask for help when they need it. Most importantly, effective communication connects them to that which inspires them.

> **ENTITLEMENT:** Believing that you are deserving of an opportunity simply because you exist. It is the enemy of empowerment.

SECURING KNOWLEDGE FROM MENTORS

It drives me crazy watching a business where there's so much knowledge and it is just going to waste. To me, knowledge is like a big bag of money. If you're not asking the people holding the purse strings to get some of that money, you're never going to get it. Most of us are great at something, yet our humility doesn't allow us to be empowered and ask other people about what they're great at, to transfer their valuable knowledge to us (and others).

Valuable knowledge can be as simple as someone's knowledge of people. Some of you may have an extraordinary amount of relationship capital. I meet these people all the time. They call themselves *connectors*. Just because you connect two people does not mean there is an exchange of value. What makes any great team great? The ones who are always asking for knowledge. Not only general managers and coaches. *Everybody* is asking for and giving help. The New England Patriots are a go-to example. Tom Brady doesn't sit on the sidelines, not sharing what he's learned about the "looks" a defense is giving and how to exploit them. He's talking with his coaches *and* his offense about what adjustments need to be made and how to execute them in quick succession. It's a system of mentoring and asking and giving help that wins the day.

One of the many books my mom made me read stands out among the rest. When I graduated from high school, I was ordered to read Ben Franklin's autobiography. I felt like that book was at least 10 inches thick. But the one thing that

I took from that book was something Franklin said: "He that has once done you a kindness will be more ready to do you another than he whom you yourself have obliged."

Humility.

Ben Franklin was saying if you have humility and ask somebody for help, that person may be more apt to help you than somebody that you've personally helped because you become an investment of that person. You have displayed humility. You have communicated effectively. You have dropped all your ego and said, "I will give you the biggest gift I can give you, one of respect." It's a gift when you ask someone for help because it is a form of that acknowledgment. You are giving that person respect for his or her decision-making acumen.

Once again, we have to start using the big bag of knowledge that you have access to through your coaching tree or relationship capital. Gain perspective from what your mentors (and mentees) know, what they've experienced. I wish I had asked more questions when I played football, instead of projecting my insecurity that I was the smallest one on the field. I could have put questions to guys like Vance Mueller, who ended up playing for the Raiders, or Christian Okoye, the "Nigerian Nightmare." Asked things like, "Hey, can you help me? Give me a few tips about how you do this. How did you get here? What should I look out for? What's the biggest mistake that you've made?"

One of the biggest keys to accelerate the benefits you receive from mentorship is relatively simple: seek out three different mentors. Whether they are all in the same arena or industry, or they have varied areas of expertise, each of your three mentors will have a unique perspective to tap into. And often, each of these individuals will have also had mentors themselves, so the amount of situational knowledge you can leverage increases exponentially as you go from one mentor to two and to three. You also improve your awareness, how perceptive you are, with this advanced level of situational knowledge.

Sometimes, all it takes to make a decision is to ask someone else one question. If you're talking to someone with situational knowledge, someone you think might help you progress in some manner, ask him or her one question, whether in person, on the phone, email or social media. There's knowledge everywhere. This is all value, yet most of the time, our egos won't allow us to ask for help.

Bill Russell is one of the most famous basketball players of all time, but he would never have gotten as far as he did without help. In 2016, he penned an article for *USA TODAY* about how important it is to have the right mentor.[2] Believe it or not, Bill was cut from his JV team as a sophomore at his high school in Oakland after only one day of tryouts. Afterward, his middle school coach walked up to a dejected Bill and heard what had happened.

His old coach, a man by the name of George Powles, was also the varsity coach, and he told Bill to come try out for varsity, despite not making the junior varsity team, and to wait for him after practice. Coach Powles took him to the local Boys & Girls Club and told him to play basketball every day—the coach knew the importance of being consistent and persistent. He even gave Bill $2 to pay for the membership to the Boys & Girls Club, understanding that this was the best path for the young man.

After being cut, had Bill not had his mentor, the NBA would not have had a 12-time All-Star, an 11-time NBA champion, and a five-time MVP of the league. Bill won two national championships at University of San Francisco, a gold medal in the 1956 Olympics, and even the Presidential Medal of Freedom. Needless to say, Bill Russell is considered by many as one of the top 10 basketball players of all time, all made possible due to the investment that Coach Powles made in a young person who might not have had access to opportunities otherwise.

Not only that, but because of Bill's experiences as a young basketball player, he understood the importance of paying it forward and sharing his situational knowledge. Bill Russell became a founding board member of Mentor, the National Mentoring Partnership. He has worked to spread mentoring membership movements, so that others can get the inspiration and support that he did as a youngster. He has also shared his situational knowledge with decades' worth of young basketball and football players, helping everyone from the NFL's Ahmad Rashad to the NBA's Kobe Bryant. He has transferred his knowledge to ensure that his mentees (and their mentees) are put in the best position to achieve their goals.

I had the opportunity to venture up to the Dreams Never Die Foundation, which was founded by CJ Anderson, Super Bowl running back for the Broncos who was cut by two teams during the 2018 NFL season before finding a home with the Los Angeles Rams and aiding them to a Super Bowl appearance. The organization provides academic and athletic mentorship and support to local youths. CJ grew up in Vallejo and went to Jesse M. Bethel High School, an area described as "crime-ridden" by many and not the best place to encourage a young man to chase big dreams. Everyone in the high school knew that CJ had great talent, but he wasn't a serious student, so he had to go to junior college.

When he went to junior college, he didn't have the spirit of excellence. His football coach was his mentor, and he had pushed him to go to junior college, telling him he believed in him, giving him more guidance. CJ took the wrong attitude to college—a negative unconscious competency, along with the wrong work ethic—and he ended up being the second-string running back. He called his coach from high school and said, "Hey, you sent me to this junior college. I'm not even starting. I think I'm going to quit."

His mentor coach said, "You're not quitting, and there's only one reason why you're not starting: because you're not grateful, you're not empathetic, you're not accountable, and you're not communicating effectively. You're not living an inspired life. You're not communicating with them. You haven't shown him a reason to start you. You're the best running back at that place, I guarantee it."

Because of his former coach's mentorship, CJ went on to become one of the best junior college running back prospects, going to Berkeley after junior college, still carrying that spirit of excellence, and later on winning a Super Bowl with the Denver Broncos and helping the Los Angeles Rams to make an appearance in Super Bowl LIII.

Now, the main thing CJ learned through this process was to be humble. His mentor allowed him to feel comfortable enough to ask for help from others and he listened. There's such a fine line in mentorship, a subtlety of success, between success and failure, between making yourself a victim and making yourself the story.

At the Dreams Never Die Foundation Football Camp that CJ runs, not only has he mentored hundreds of aspiring young athletes, but he has been joined in his efforts by the football coach who'd been there 40 years, the professional baseball player from Vallejo, a former Raider, guys who had played at schools like Florida and Florida State . . . the list goes on and on. They've all come back knowing the value they received from great mentors, and they've all wanted to pay it forward. The little kids at the camp wear shirts with three numbers on the back: 32–254–22. The numbers are a reminder that despite being great on the California Golden Bears team for the University of California, Berkeley, there were 32 teams that CJ wasn't drafted by, 254 players who were drafted instead of him, and 22 running backs who were drafted instead of him. A lot of people were chosen ahead of him, yet he was the starting running back beside Peyton Manning on a Super Bowl–winning team, and he is still in the NFL today.

That doesn't happen without the productivity and accessibility of mentorship. Being a mentor and being able to be mentored. In this mentorship, you need to harness the knowledge, you need to harness the skills, and you need to harness the desire and the inspiration through gratitude, empathy, and accountability. That will guide you on your path in a more efficient, effective, and statistically successful way.

PROFITING FROM THE BEST COACHES (OR THEIR COACHING TREE)

Apart from his countless on-the-field successes, one of the things that legendary coach Bill Parcells is known for is his coaching tree. Heading into the 2018 NFL season, 29 of the 32 NFL head coaches can be connected to Bill Parcells's coaching tree, many through his connections to fellow coaching legends like Bill Belichick and Nick Saban. There are 12 Super Bowl rings between his protégés Belichick, Tom Coughlin, and Sean Payton alone. And each of the 12 NFL head coaches who made the NFL Playoffs in the 2018 season were connected to Parcells or the father of the West Coast offense, Bill Walsh.[3]

In an interview before his Hall of Fame induction, Coach Parcells said, "You, as an individual coach, have a responsibility to try to give those players who put themselves at risk and in harm's way a chance to achieve success."[4]

We all put ourselves in the way of risks. We all put ourselves in the way of harm. If others' knowledge can help reduce the likelihood of either, then why aren't you focused on helping others or asking mentors for help? Parcells did a great job putting his team in a position to succeed and win, which is why he's in the Hall of Fame. He would always point out that blame, shame, and justification did no good for a team. He instilled in his team that pointing out problems without working to solve them was useless. A simple waste of energy. A prime example of this for "Big Tuna" came when Parcells was frustrated with Lawrence Taylor (LT) because he wasn't following Parcells's defensive scheme, so he took it upon himself to make an adjustment. Parcells built his defensive scheme around the uber-talented linebacker instead, which led to the Big Blue Wrecking Crew, as the defense was known, leading the Giants to two Super Bowl wins in the 1980s.

Here are some quotes from Parcells's book *Finding a Way to Win: The Principles of Leadership, Teamwork and Motivation,* that I feel are particularly invocative of a need for humility.[5]

"*A good teacher creates an environment which allows the student to succeed.*" Humility is not intuitive, so you need to create an environment where humility is intuitive. One of the strategies I have used is to give a Dummy Tax Award. To be clear, this award has not been given this name because the person making the mistake is a dummy. It's because those same mistakes have been made by others before him or her, and the mistakes can almost always be avoided simply by asking for help. Only dummies pay taxes twice, however. We present these awards at a companywide meeting where we go around the room and share a mistake that we've made in the last month that has most affected the company, as well as whether the mistake was made because of a lack of gratitude, empathy, accountability, effective communication, or a combination.

> **DUMMY TAX:** The cost of a mistake that could have been avoided using the situational knowledge of others who have faced a similar decision.

By sharing that value, it's like I'm opening the purse strings of the big bag of situational knowledge to anyone willing to take part in the exercise. Everyone can hear and learn, but it also takes great humility to be vulnerable enough to admit bad decisions and their root cause, especially around coworkers. For the team to be motivated to be honest, humble, and grounded, a financial incentive, such as a $500 bonus, is sometimes needed.

Before I put that financial incentive in place, people were less eager to admit mistakes. They would say they forgot to remind someone of a phone call. Or they didn't volunteer to work at an event. With $500 dollars in play, they were jumping at the chance to share how they really screwed up. Many possibilities open up if you can create an environment for humility. It's been done by many a football squad. In fact, among the many things of note about Bill Parcells' Super Bowl teams is that they were not allowed to celebrate anything until after the game. This was not due to a taunting rule or a celebration rule. It was simply humility. It was gratitude. They were taught to score that touchdown, hand the ball to the referee, and say thank you. They acted like they'd been there before and carried an energy of humility with every action they took.

"Accept false steps as opportunities to learn. It's one thing to hate failure; it's another to fear it." I love that quote from Parcells because fearing failure creates a void of failure that will be filled, eventually. It attracts more failure. I hate failure because it can cause momentary frustration, but I also love it because building something using blocks of failure helps you step up to success. Without failure, you can't learn and move forward as a decision maker. Don't fear it. Welcome it. If you're not failing, you're not trying. You're living in some comfort zone. You're not expanding.

Failure is as certain as taxes. And it definitely is as certain as death. So, why fear it? You're wasting energy being afraid of failing or you're attracting what you don't want: failure. Know that as you're failing, you're learning. To avoid repeating these mistakes, think about who you could have asked to save yourself from what happened. Humility is truly what makes a great mentee and a great mentor.

"A team divided against itself, can break down at any moment. The least bit of pressure or adversity will crack it apart." The same applies to an individual. You put a group under pressure, and if it's not united, it's going to fall apart. Put a person under pressure who doesn't have a perspective of gratitude, empathy, accountability, and effective communication, and he or she will fall apart.

I always say that when you put a team under pressure, it's just like an orange. When you squeeze an orange, what comes out of that orange? Orange juice. Why does orange juice come out of an orange when you squeeze? Because that's what's inside of it. What happens to a company when under pressure? You discover what's truly inside of it. You don't find out what's inside of you when you're excelling and everything is going fine. If you lose everything, I guarantee you'll find out what's inside of you. Because once you figure out what's inside of you, you can change it.

POSTGAME WRAP-UP

Empowering your team to find the right mentors to coach them starts with their capacity for humility—that is, being able to ask for help from others. This goes for leaders as well as team members. Mentorship is a two-way street that creates a system of accountability when it is put in place in an organization, accelerating the learning process for all involved and making your entire team better in the process.

Identify mentors by paying attention to the skills and knowledge that they bring to the table. Those humble enough to ask will learn about the successes and mistakes of their mentors, sharpening their decision-making skills in the process. Mentors can use their situational knowledge to guide their mentees through tough situations, propelling them toward personal and professional growth at a rapid pace.

4

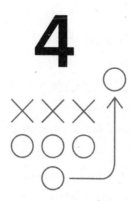

Don't Trip on the First-Down Chains Behind You

PREGAME ANALYSIS

Your past should inform your decision making, but you cannot let your perspective of the past interfere with your future progress. An overreliance on your past can cause issues with your ego, such as a lack of forgiveness, that will unduly influence your decisions going forward and impair your ability to make the right call. Like a young quarterback, you need to have the right approach to "the game" in order to excel, regardless of any pressure that is put on you or pressure you might put on yourself.

Whether facing a time crunch or attempting to recover from a mistake, the perspective that you take about your past successes and failures will either promote future triumph or attract disappointment. Learn to overcome your past struggles by adopting a mistake response (a routine reaction to deal with any missteps and errors you make) that will help you stay centered in your core values and avoid the pitfalls of ego. Whether you made the right call or the wrong call on your last drive, you always need to be prepared to make the *next* call.

When I talk about time, I talk about how it affects your perception in the present. That perception is directly related to your attitude and how you consciously take in information and subconsciously hold on to that information, which then attracts new information and establishes an unconscious competency—that is, the energy you carry.

Due to our perception of time, many of us are stuck in the past. I used to say, "Don't stumble on the roadblocks behind you." This perspective, however, accounts for only the negativity that is behind us. Now I tell my team, "Don't trip on the first-down chains behind you"—because first downs can be achieved in two ways: you either get a first down or fail on fourth down, giving your opponent a new set of downs.

I see the perception of our past as a huge problem in business, and this can be seen in the three realms of belief. We consciously trip on the first-down chains behind us by focusing too much on our past failures, shortcomings, or anxieties. Other times, subconsciously or unconsciously, we hold on to beliefs that are limiting. How many of us feel limited by what our parents have told us? Or what coaches have told us? There are even cases in which we are limited by what we tell ourselves.

When I started thinking about my perception and the relativity of time, I thought back to when I was a little boy and wanted to be a millionaire. A million dollars, to me, was an incredible amount of money. My perception at five years old was that if I were a millionaire, I would have no problems in life. This perception has completely changed now that I've had the experience of making millions of dollars in a given day. Now, I look at people and I think, somebody out there is making a hundred billion dollars. And there are companies out there that are losing a hundred billion dollars! That wasn't even imaginable to me as a young man, which is why my desire for a million dollars sat in my subconscious. That was a limiting belief for me. To this day, I am challenging myself constantly to rid my subconscious of limiting beliefs so that these ideas don't become an unconscious competency. The only way for any of us to identify such beliefs is to raise our awareness of them.

STUDY THE PAST: HUMAN NATURE NEVER CHANGES

Studying history or the past is one way to raise this awareness. There's a difference between stumbling on the first-down chains behind you and *studying* the first-down chains behind you. A huge difference! Studying history is essential for only one reason, to learn human nature. I love to study history to elevate my awareness about human action and emotion. I love to study my history, as well as other people's history, because human nature never changes. What doesn't change about human nature are two variables that cause us to get in our own way (or to get out of it): time and ego.

Let's talk about the relationship between time and perception. Factually, our past remains the same, but it's our perception of the past that really matters. I look back, and there was a time when my bankruptcy was the most embarrassing, shameful, terrible thing that had ever happened to me. The fact remained that in 2009, I claimed bankruptcy and lost every single thing that I had, and my perception for a long time was that my bankruptcy was a terrible ill.

Why is it that, a decade later, it's the best thing that ever happened to me? Factually, nothing has changed. My bankruptcy still exists. It didn't go away. What has changed is the way I illuminate the experience and use it to teach people to think, say, and do the right things when it comes to their relationship with money. I find that people ask me more questions about how my bankruptcy happened and how I persevered than questions about anything else. That's because they want to leverage my firsthand experiences. How many things in our past do we have the wrong perceptions of, and how quickly can we change our perception?

Have you ever been upset, and then only moments later, somehow not been upset about something that happened in the past? That happens to all of us. Sometimes it's because we realize we're wrong. Other times, we've gotten additional data, which has changed our original feelings or actions. Whatever the impetus for this change in emotion, it comes from an ability to forgive ourselves (or others) when we approach the past as a "Monday morning quarterback." Has the past changed? No, the past has remained the same. It's our perception of the past that has changed. And, regardless, with gratitude, empathy, accountability, and effective communication, we can quickly get back to our center where we don't have the wrong perception of the past. The past is a miracle. The past is a miracle because it provides the lessons we need to pursue our potential in the future.

As you look at time, you can see that the present is totally different, and so will be the future because of your perception. Fernando Pessoa wrote in *The Book of Disquiet*, "My past is everything I failed to be." In other words, the past provides you an indicator of what potential you have. It's just a lesson. The lesson is in asking, "Where did I fall short of my potential?" There's no good, no bad, no judgments or conditions on this answer, unless you create them. Only a lesson (or two) to learn from, so that you can continue to enjoy the pursuit of your potential.

To look for where we have failed to reach our potential is a very positive perspective to have, and it's relative to our higher self, which is the truth. We have potential in a countless number of areas. It could be as a leader or coach, father or mother, son or daughter, or as a family member. It could be as a businessperson—our economic potential. Not everybody has the same potential. I have only a certain potential in jumping high or playing basketball. I have a different potential in running fast. Everyone has different potential in different areas, but the enjoyment of the pursuit of our potential, regardless of what that potential is, is truly what creates happiness. And happiness is the key to life.

If the past is everything you failed to be, then the future will allow for your growth, both personally and professionally. The future is better than the past, in the respect that you have the opportunity to pursue your potential while learning from the past. Remember, your higher self lives in the truth, and you live in relativity to the truth. So, the key to a positive perspective (one of thinking that your past is everything that you failed to be) is trusting that everything will come to you in the right way at the perfect time. Understand that time is not linear. If you're waiting for something or if you put an arbitrary deadline on something, you are creating resistance, and so it's going to take longer to get there.

What if you could take time out of your perception? How could you make that decision consciously, and then, eventually, unconsciously? It's simple. Enjoy the pursuit of your potential. If you look back to the past to inform your future, start looking at where you failed to reach your potential and what you learned from it. All of a sudden, you'll enjoy the past more than you did previously, and you'll be more excited about the future because it's an opportunity to reach your potential. This decision-making perspective is all about the energy that you put into it. Understanding time and attaching time to your perception is a really important component of not stumbling over the first-down markers behind you, be they positive or negative.

ZONE COVERAGE: THE COMFORT, LEARNING, AND ANXIETY ZONES

It's so important to find your center when you think about time and find a positive, calm place to make decisions from, away from any anxiety you feel about your past. When things don't feel right when making decisions, take the step to identify when you are in your comfort zone, learning zone, or anxiety zone. Like a pitcher with a full count, you want to be in the right part of the zone to best enjoy the pursuit of your potential. You can't do that when you're in a comfort zone, and you can't do that when you're in an anxiety zone. You can enjoy the pursuit of your potential only when you're in the learning zone.

The question is, how are these zones relative to your ego? The relativity of your ego can cause you to feel a need to be separate, inferior, or superior in relation to those who are around you, all due to your inability to forgive yourself for past actions. The ego is what takes us out of the learning zone and puts us into the anxiety zone, or it can put us back into a comfort zone.

Over the years, I've seen countless people who were pushing themselves so hard physically, mentally, and emotionally that they were living their life in an anxiety zone. Then, all of a sudden, things started to become overwhelming. They couldn't learn anything new because they were besieged by the stress of current actions. In fact, I've seen people who had nervous breakdowns, pushing themselves so hard in anxiety zones that the anxiety became a comfort zone. What does that mean? They could take only those actions that were unconscious or subconscious. They were paralyzed by fear. They stayed in bed all day. They couldn't physically get out of bed. They were too fatigued to do anything, much less make a sound decision. They had shrunk their comfort zone by pursuing their potential without perspective or enjoyment.

Their rampant ego meant that they had lost their gratitude and forgiveness. Their ego was causing them to feel fear, guilt, and shame over past mistakes, missteps, and bad decisions. They weren't looking at the past as a miracle.

I look at every lesson I have learned as a miracle. Even the toughest ones, like declaring bankruptcy. It's so valuable for you to understand that successive events are just additional steps toward your potential. It is the needs of your ego that cause you to react in opposition to things instead of being aware enough to make the right move. You shouldn't have to react to anything. The only reaction that you should have is to go back to your decision-making center.

So many times, we have a situation that takes us out of our learning zone, and we go into the **anxiety zone**, which is the zone of the ego where we experience fear, anxiety, shame, guilt, or any mix of those feelings. And then we go ahead and exacerbate it by resisting it and fighting against the situation instead of working with it. Making justifications instead of taking accountability. Instead, we need to realize that our goal when we're in the anxiety zone is to first come back to center. We need to keep in mind that with respect to time, this situation that we are currently facing is just a lesson.

> **ANXIETY ZONE:** An area of your life where making a decision causes a perceived pressure, shortage, or obstacle to action.

Champions take the belief that there's not one thing that happens to us that doesn't put us in a better place to get what we want, even though it may not feel like it when we're in the middle of a struggle. The challenge becomes whether or not we have the perspective to go back to center so that we can appreciate these lessons quicker. If we're honest, there are many times of the day when we are not living in our truth or living to our potential. That's one reason I ask a lot of people what advice they have for me when interacting with those who have pursued their potential and attained situational knowledge in different areas than I have.

I was told that one morning when we were all in the office, my door was closed and I was yelling at somebody on the phone and swearing at him, and the people I work with could hear me through the door. And I admitted my mistake. I needed a thicker door. Of course, the true lesson for me was to mind how quickly I could go back to center, even when I was dealing with a frustrating call.

How quickly you can get back to center is how fast you can expand your learning and comfort zones when it comes to making decisions. The problem with the ego is that it works not only against forgiveness but also against accountability. If you're in a space of ego, you're not accountable. Your ego makes you a victim of the past instead of making the past your story. How many people do you know talk about being that victim? Some of the most successful people on earth have persevered through difficult times. But in the mindset of victims, a feeling of powerlessness can take over, paralyzing them into perpetual indecision, which can be worse than making a bad decision.

GRATITUDE

You use four values—gratitude, empathy, accountability, and effective communication—to give yourself a positive perspective on difficulties in deciding on the best way to go, which heightens your awareness and empowers you to act or go back to center. Gratitude is a simple solution that gives you a great perspective of your past, present, and future. It's simple. This is one of the straightforward lessons you can learn, to coach yourself if you go off-center due to ego or if time constraints or arbitrary deadlines cause you to feel rushed. When you think about not making enough money or about needing to be further along in meeting a goal, your ego comes into play. Gratitude changes that immediately, telling you that you're right where you're supposed to be at the perfect time.

Does gratitude stop you from working hard? Absolutely not. In fact, I believe gratitude makes you work harder. Makes you work smarter and happier. Allows you to enjoy the pursuit of your potential, consistently, every day. Two words can change your life: *thank you*. Just say "thank you" before you go to bed and when you wake up. Watch how quickly your life changes. Do it for 30 straight days—that's all you need. I challenge you to say "thank you" when difficulties occur. When you feel as if you haven't reached your potential and face a difficult task, saying "thank you" will enlighten you and make you aware. When you feel that the universe is unjust, you can change everything with gratitude. Saying "thank you" will allow the awareness of the lesson to come quicker.

I'm not telling you not to grab onto your dreams and do everything you can to make them a reality. I'm asking you to enjoy the pursuit of your potential and be humble enough to understand that you don't know the way to get there. You might not know how or what to live by in order to make it so, but know it's going to happen. When things don't go the way you think they're supposed to go or how you planned them to go, allow what's supposed to happen to happen. You don't have to be right. You live in the favor of the universe—so start trusting!

For those of you who are still uncertain about this trust, give the following parable your attention, and hopefully, you will better understand the need to accept your current situation with gratitude and be empowered to take action. Allowing you to move forward with confidence.

TRUSTING ENOUGH TO LET GO OF EGO

I'm that guy sitting on a ledge, looking over, testing my fear, because everyone's afraid of something. Just testing it, leaning over. Do you ever do that on a tall building or a bridge, and you get a weird feeling in your stomach? You aren't falling, but you're afraid of falling, so your ego is telling you, "No, your body isn't going to handle flying 300 feet into rocks and water. Be careful."

But what if you resist while persisting, and you fall over? This is a story about a guy who leans over, and he falls, and on the way down, about 10 feet down, he gets caught up in some tree branches and he grabs on. So, now he's hanging there, 200 and some feet below, and he looks up, and he says, "Is anybody up there? Is anybody up there who can help me?" And the universe yells down, "Yeah, I can help you. Let go. I'll catch you."

Now, most people would hang onto that branch with all their might. Including me, in the past. I'd have hung onto that branch with my life, and I'd have yelled back, "Is there anybody else who can help me? Is there any other way to go? Cuz' this letting-go thing's not gonna work for me! I don't trust it."

This was how I used to think. Initially, when I went bankrupt, I felt like I was hanging on for dear life, trying to keep as many of my assets I could, and my wife was saying, "Let go. Don't worry." And I thought, "I have three daughters. They're all gonna want to go to college, go to graduate school, get married, and who knows what else. I don't even own a house. I lost all my furniture! And you want me just to let go? Shouldn't I hang on to everything that I have?"

It wasn't easy to stop fighting against the inevitable bankruptcy. But the freedom I felt when letting go was amazing.

Think about how many times the universe is telling you, "Let go" and you resist. Your plan is a good plan. It might not end up where you think you're going to end up. It might end up way past it. What if I could make everyone who worked for me $10 million? I'm going to work and enjoy the pursuit of my potential. To make money, help people, and have fun. And I'm going to be aware of all these lessons, and when the lessons come, I have two simple words for the lesson: *thank you.*

FACTORING IN FORGIVENESS AND ACCOUNTABILITY

The second value is forgiveness, empathy. You want to stay centered? The first step is to forgive yourself. No living in blame, shame, justification. I have so many people I coach now, and it's so fun because they're in these situations with business partners, life partners, and other human relationships that are not going well, and there's a lot of baggage, history, human nature, blame. It's awful. And I'll give them this simple advice: "Forgive yourself."

I used to tell people that I don't forgive people because they deserve it. I forgive them because I deserve it. Forgiveness is so powerful. It's powerful beyond even just making yourself feel better, like saying thank you. "When you forgive, you in no way change the past, but you're sure to change the future." That's from my great-uncle, Bernard Meltzer.

It's amazing, when I coach people, that so many of them need to be reminded to forgive themselves. *Forgive yourself.* Pray for the happiness of those who wronged you. You don't have to forgive them or what they did. *Forgive yourself.* You're the one who's supposed to learn from it. If you shift the energy that way, being accepting instead of defensive, it's impossible for there to be an attack on you because you can't attack what isn't there. You can't attack a team through the air or on the ground if they don't even field a team to compete against you. We don't realize that, but the minute we defend ourselves, we create an attack. *Forgive yourself.* It'll be amazing how quickly your relationships with others (and yourself) heal.

Accountability is the third value. It forces you to be in a perspective that asks, "What did I do to attract this to myself, or what am I supposed to learn from it?" Think about the enjoyment of the pursuit of your potential and how accountability fits directly into that. If you're accountable, then you're enjoying the pursuit of your potential. If you're not making mistakes, you're not expanding. You're sitting in the comfort zone. But if you live in a learning zone, you make mistakes. I doubt there is anyone reading this book that hasn't made a mistake today. If we're being honest with ourselves, one hundred percent of us have already made a mistake before lunchtime almost every day of our lives.

Imagine, if you're not gracious about the enjoyment of the pursuit of your potential. Imagine if you're not forgiving, and imagine if you're not accountable. How difficult would it be to deal with the mistakes of others, or your own? Now, the question is, how often are we gracious, empathetic, and accountable? How quickly are we grateful, empathetic, and accountable?

When we are gracious, empathetic, and accountable, we can connect emotionally, which in turn enables us to communicate effectively. So many times, we trip over what's behind us, the first-down marker, because we don't communicate effectively. So the more that we can connect emotionally, the quicker we can collect emotionally. The time we save is a major factor when it comes to effective decision making and success.

PRESSURE AND PERSPECTIVE

Have you ever been late for an appointment or late for a phone call? Do you ever feel actual anxiety or pressure when that happens? Ask yourself whether the anxiety and pressure help you be on time, or if they usually create resistance that slows you down. It's amazing what happens when you start putting yourself under needless strain.

So much energy is wasted on the negative. Faith isn't just about putting faith in the positive. People put faith in the negative and then they're surprised when there's negative, right? They put faith in what they *don't have* . . . and they get more of what they don't have.

Positive and negative. People waste energy on the negative. You should enjoy the pursuit of your potential, which means that whether in your opinion you experience a positive or negative outcome, you should try just to keep an enjoyment of it. The most successful teams and players in all sports not only enjoy their jobs, but are able to maintain an even keel in the tough times, as well as the times of prosperity. This is done by keeping emotions in check, no matter if you've got a massive lead or deficit in the game you're playing. Your emotions need to be as consistent as possible. Not too low, not too high. That took me a long time to learn. Not to get too mad, get back to center fast, without wasting much energy.

How do you have the most energy possible? Just don't waste it. I've got the same amount of energy you have. I don't waste it when I sleep, I don't waste it on being angry, I don't waste it on my ego, I don't waste it on time. I catch myself when I'm putting energy into something unnecessary. I don't want to waste energy because the more energy I have, the more I can do, the more action I can take, the more people I can help, the more money I can make. And where does that drive come from? Communicating effectively with what inspires me and connecting emotionally with others.

There are two approaches to coaching others, in general. The first approach is to manipulate people. You can manipulate other people, lie to yourself, and not pursue your true potential. The other approach is to motivate others, inspire them with your words and actions. To succeed at this, you need to use your energy to connect to that which inspires you. Connect to the enjoyment of the pursuit of your potential. That's what energy should be used for, to reach your potential. If I have more energy than you, I'll have a better capability of reaching my potential than you have, even if I have fewer skills and less knowledge. If I have more energy, I'll be better able to reach my potential. That energy is used for inspiration, and inspiration is a higher vibration that allows you to effectuate the truth.

Can you be sad if you're inspired?

Think about it.

You can't.

Can't be depressed. Can't be sad. Not when inspired. There's very little that happens other than good things when you're inspired. Have you ever experienced being inspired and it seems like time flies? When we're uninspired, how long does time take? Inspiration is a critical component of learning and growing, which is why it is so essential to understand how and when we learn, when we experience anxiety and stress, and when we are simply doing what we are accustomed to.

THE COMFORT ZONE

We start with your comfort zone, which could also be called the "riding-the-bike zone." Some people would love to live their life in the comfort zone, but I believe it's an uninspired place. Are you inspired to go ride your bike? Professional cyclists may be, but for most of us, this activity can be done with unconscious effort. The necessity to breathe in and out is not very inspiring, but you breathe. There are some things that are so comfortable for us to do that they come naturally, without thought and without taking us off-center.

Unsure of the importance of being centered when it comes to efficient and effective decisions? Well, imagine a martial arts sensei who sits in the middle of a circle of 10 to 15 people, and he has them attack him, and he defends against each aggressor until he is the only one left standing. How does he take on so many attacks at one time? I think some people can see a parallel in the way they approach their day. They feel the same thing. How are they dealing with all of this stuff at one time? There's no reaction from the master, that's why.

I used to think that the martial arts master reacted very quickly. However, what he's doing is what we all want to do, which is key to the enjoyment of the pursuit of potential, key to not tripping on the first-down markers behind us. Simply put, to look forward, we actually just go back—not back in history, but back to center. The learning zone is actually the center. Something happens that puts you in the anxiety zone? Analogously that's like one of the enemies coming to attack. When something happens, you need to return to your center in order to make a confident decision. You need to take yourself out of time and ego because time and ego are the two things that waste the energy that you have. Time will put pressure on you. Ego will put pressure on you.

THE LEARNING ZONE

How do you take off the ego and time pressures? What will happen is that if you keep this philosophy of gratitude, empathy, accountability, and effective communication, pretty soon your learning zone will become the size of your comfort zone. There are all these things that just go on that you don't have to think about. It's just like riding a bike. It takes no energy at all to execute. It just happens.

What used to make me crazy, and anxious, with time and ego pressures has now become my learning zone. I can handle it, no problem at all. If I keep on living with gratitude, empathy, accountability, and effective communication, then I will stop tripping over the first-down markers in the past and simply stay present with gratitude, empathy, and accountability. Pretty soon, my anxiety zone will shrink and my comfort zone will expand.

The comfort zone is the area that you know like the back of your hand, and it takes no thought at all. It is made up of your conscious and unconscious competencies, things that you can execute on with minimal effort or attention. Your comfort zone encompasses your decisions that you regularly make and that you're 100 percent confident in.

You need to have a learning zone outside of your comfort zone because it will allow you to expand and learn how to make harder and more complex decisions. Expand your comfort zone, the way a butterfly breaking out of a cocoon strengthens its wings so it can fly. You need to stay in your learning zone as much as possible so that the comfort zone grows and grows and you can handle more and more.

What I'm conscious about in my comfort zone is that it's continually expanding, that I'm not constricting my comfort zone. I'd be very wary if something that was in my comfort zone all of a sudden made me anxious. For example, I got to speak in front of 24,000 people at the 2018 RISE Conference in Hong Kong, and my daughter asked me if I was going to be nervous.

I said, "Why would I be nervous? I'll put you on stage, and I'll ask you to clap. Would you be nervous?"

She said no. Why? Because clapping's in her comfort zone. It takes very little thought to decide to clap, right? And no matter how many people there are, if I asked her to do what she's comfortable with, she can do it.

I've learned that if I'm going to stand in front of people, I want to be in my comfort zone. When I'm performing, I don't want to be in a learning zone. If I'm performing something new, I need to have practiced it so much that my comfort zone has expanded. I need to have learned it enough that it has now entered my comfort zone. One of the NBA's greatest free throw shooters, Steve Nash, is a perfect example of this. If you've ever seen him shoot free throws, you'll notice one thing: he practices his shot before the refs even hand him the ball. Not only is this routine part of his comfort zone, it is ingrained in his subconscious and unconscious. And the results are inarguable; he was the most efficient free throw shooter of all time before being (barely) overtaken by Stephen Curry.

There's also a second side of decision making in certain circumstances when time and ego would be in place. Why does it really matter how many people are out there when I'm on the stage? It's simply ego, because I am afraid to embarrass myself. I'm afraid that I won't connect with 24,000 people. I'm afraid that I'll feel inferior when I'm onstage. That's the only reason I'd be nervous.

If I hold on to the fear, and I don't go back to center, then I'm guaranteed only one thing: I've put faith in the fear that I won't be enough. And guess what? It'll make me more nervous. And if I'm nervous, it'll be more difficult to connect to 24,000 people. You can see how this all works together, and it's all either time or ego based. Those decisions in the comfort zone are easy decisions, but they still have to be made.

The learning zone isn't exclusive to academics, obviously. There's learning in everything you do, whether you're a rookie or a veteran. It's where you can appreciate the lessons that the universe gives you. It's the enjoyment of the pursuit of your potential. It's where we live. It's where we practice, making well-informed decisions. You can't learn to make tough decisions unless you have one of two things: either you have to have firsthand experience of it, or you have to ask others who have situational knowledge of or actual experience in a similar situation. The learning zone is the place where the three (at least) mentors that you should always have will live.

THE ANXIETY ZONE

It's important to know when you're stuck in the comfort zone or when you're not challenging yourself. You should also know that when you're in the anxiety zone, you're pushing yourself too hard, which is just as bad as being in the comfort zone. This happens all the time. People get in their own way. They're perceiving that they're not getting done in time, they don't have enough time, or things aren't happening fast enough. They keep worrying about what they're going to do next. It's all time and ego, which leads to fear.

It's great to make decisions in the learning zone with gratitude, empathy, accountability, and effective communication because you actually know that you're learning. Everybody who is reading this has made a mistake already today, but some of us are too afraid of making the next mistake. Why not enjoy the mistakes? Isn't it a lot simpler than tripping on the first-down markers behind you?

The book that describes fear to me the best is one of my all-time favorite books. The Sesame Street book *The Monster at the End of This Book: Starring Lovable, Furry Old Grover* is a fantastic story about not creating anxiety. It starts off with

Grover saying, be careful because there is a monster at the end of this book, warning that whatever you do, don't turn the page.

Of course, you turn the page, and then Grover's on the second page. He warns you again that there's a monster at the end of this book, and he threatens to nail the page up so you can't turn it. You turn the page, and it's been "boarded up" everywhere, with Grover standing there, even more horrified and afraid, way out in the anxiety zone. He warns you again about a monster at the end of the book, this time telling you that he's going to brick it up. You turn the page, and it's been "bricked up." This continues until eventually you get to the end of the book. You turn the last page, and guess who's there? Grover. He says, "Oh, my gosh, I'm the monster at the end of the book. Lovable, cuddly Grover."

How many times do we do that to ourselves, creating unnecessary anxiety and worry? Not making decisions in the learning zone because we're afraid there's a monster. We need to be saying, "I can't wait to see what's on the next page!"

I know that we make mistakes going through our progression as decision makers, but know that each page you turn is putting you closer to your potentials, regardless of what you think those potentials are. You need to know when you're pushing yourself too hard, meaning with time and ego. It's okay if you can't get it done. There's always tomorrow. That doesn't mean you're not enjoying the pursuit to get it done, but don't slow yourself down because of time, and definitely don't slow yourself down because of ego. There's no monster at the end of the book. There's just you.

Outside of your learning zone is that anxiety zone. The good thing about the anxiety zone is that it allows you to know when you're pushing yourself too hard. I love to live my life right there on the border of that zone and the learning zone. When I feel a crossover, where I go deeper into the anxiety zone, I come back. I attempt to never make a conscious decision in the anxiety zone. Why would I do that to myself? Why would I want to run a race with no tennis shoes on or, even worse, drive a car race with only three tires? That's anxiety. Am I ever going to win consistently in that situation? No way!

The only lesson you learn from making a decision when you're in the anxiety zone is *don't make decisions when you're in the anxiety zone.* Instead, first go back to the learning zone, then make the decision. How quickly can you get back to the learning zone? That's the sole decision to make when you're in the anxiety zone.

Know that being consistently in the anxiety zone is no way to operate. You need to take accountability for the decisions you make, and you need to be ready to learn. Once again, gratitude, empathy, accountability, and effective communication will take you back to the learning zone. It'll keep you out of the comfort zone when your perspective is that of desiring growth, and then you'll be continually expanding your comfort zone in the process. Over time, doing that will expand your learning zone, which will create a whole new anxiety zone to test the boundaries of. It's also just as important to be aware when you're in the comfort zone and not doing anything, not taking any action, as it is important to be aware when you're taking too much action.

RESPONDING TO MISTAKES

When it comes to some of the toughest positions in sports, like quarterbacks or defensive backs in football, or pitchers in baseball, there's often talk of having a short memory. In baseball, obviously pitchers have to have a short memory. It's only a matter of time until they hang a ball in the zone that ends up as a home run. Quarterbacks throw balls dozens of times per game, and getting intercepted (or fumbling due to blindside hits from the defense) is always part of the game. But they can't dwell on it. And as a team, football players can't dwell on their losses, because putting faith in what you don't want will only result in more of the same.

I love the beginning of the NFL season because there are so many teams that go 0–2, and the fans all overreact, crying, "It's the end of our season." It's not. There are lots of different circumstances in which you should stay right in the learning zone instead of forfeiting to the anxiety zone after a poor start, and there are plenty of 14–2 teams, or 13–3 teams, or even 10–6 teams that win Super Bowls. Even 9–7 teams win the big game occasionally. So, 2 losses are not the end of the world. The same is true when you start out hot with your decisions. Countless teams who have started 2–0 have failed to make the playoffs. And there have even been teams like the 2009 Denver Broncos, who won their first six games to start the NFL season before going 2–8 their next ten games and failing to make the playoffs with an 8–8 record.[1] No matter the start you have, chasing consistent improvement is the only way to get the results you desire.

A majority of quarterbacks who are high on the all-time passes list are also high on the all-time interceptions list. And corners and safeties cover some of the biggest, quickest, and fastest athletes on the planet. They have to accept getting beaten as part of the game and make adjustments to their plan. Pitchers can't let a poor pitch selection or location or even a good hitter get in their head. They need to accept their mistake and understand it is a part of the learning zone.

To avoid biased or tilted decision making, you need to work on creating an appropriate **mistake response**, which is simply a strategy to help you go back to the learning zone. Imagine throwing a pitch and saying thank you when the guy hits a home run off of you—and forgiving yourself. People smirk when I say that, but think about it in those terms.

> **MISTAKE RESPONSE:** A pattern or habit ingrained by the way that you respond to making an error in judgment. A healthy mistake response can prepare you to avoid future mistakes, while a negative mistake response can put you into a slump.

Somebody hits a home run off of you. Are you more likely to pitch the next batter better if you get mad at yourself, if you get mad at the catcher, mad at the coach, or get mad at the batter? Or do you think you might have a better chance if you say thank you and forgive yourself? Think about how many people fail to do that in their business or home life. We all know we'd do better, but our own ego, our innate sense, prevents us from responding with positivity. We should train that habit.

You should say thank you after pitching off a home run. You should be thankful after hitting the batter. You should be thankful after throwing an interception. You should do this for only one reason: if you're thankful, forgiving, accountable, and communicating effectively with what inspires you, then you have a much better chance to continue the game and win.

Do you know what **the yips** are? Most golfers usually do, but the yips are seen in all sports. It's the actual loss of motor skills that athletes experience when they feel a large amount of pressure (usually time and ego are the two pressures), which causes them to be unable to execute the smallest tasks. It occurs due to ego being in the way—it happens when everyone's focused on the athlete. The athlete is afraid of being embarrassed in front of all these people.

THE YIPS: The inability to take a simple action or make a split-second call due to an imagined fear of repercussion.

How many great athletes have failed in front of millions of people? The answer is, "All of them." Michael Jordan is one of the greatest athletes of all time, and in the book *Nike Culture: The Sign of the Swoosh*[2] he counts his lessons. He says that he was asked to take the final shot 26 times and he missed. But he swung back to the learning zone. Nobody thinks that Michael Jordan's a loser. And I promise you, Michael Jordan has failed at something already today. But he never quits (except temporarily to play baseball).

In golf, players often struggle with the yips. You see countless golfers who would play better if they had just said thank you while they made mistakes, instead of living in the anxiety zone. Typically, a golfer with the yips tends to struggle to make even the simplest putts. Too anxious to do what they need to do and what they've trained their entire life to do.

When you're in that anxiety zone, even stuff that you normally do in the comfort zone now becomes challenging. Indecision in business is often compared to the yips because it isn't about making a correct choice, but rather, it's about being blocked from taking action or hedging against potential failures. You're not taking a learning action, and you're afraid to see a no.

One of my favorite things I teach is this: What if I told you that you're only 25 nos away from what you want? How excited would you be at your first refusal? Your second no. Your third no. What if I told you you're only 25 nos from being successful at what you're trying to do in business? How would you feel after your twentieth no?

A lot different from someone who didn't believe that she was only 25 nos away.

I guarantee you that in business, you're only so many nos away from getting what you want. You should be just as excited as if you knew there were only 25 of them. Don't quit. Just learn and keep learning. Fear often causes indecision and inaction in decision making because it is a deep-seated adaptive drive for survival and self-preservation. You need to take action.

The fear inflicted by ego puts you in your own way, creating doubt and indecision, which want you to revert back to your comfort zone. For an achiever, perhaps the most dangerous, most destructive habit of all is procrastination. Procrastination is fear based. There's no other reason than that not to do something now, when you are capable of doing it, other than fear-based, ego-based decision making. When you put things off once, it's easier to put them off again, until the habit is so firmly ingrained that it cannot be easily broken.

Sadly, the effects of the procrastination habit are also cumulative. Its cure is obvious: action. You'll be surprised how quickly you'll begin to feel better about yourself and your situation when you get going on something. Anything. Action may not always bring happiness, but there's no happiness without action. These yips are a lack of confidence in your actions—they're a state of mind that comes from you not forgiving yourself for making an error in judgment. Paralysis and procrastination are caused by fear.

You're like a golfer who does not trust that he has the right line to the cup or faith in his decisions, resulting in more misses.

Steve Sax was one of my favorite Dodgers of all time, but at one point in his career, it seemed like he could not throw the ball from second base. He was so far in the anxiety zone that doing something that should've been in his comfort zone—throwing the ball from second base to first base—was now extremely hard to do. Jon Lester of the Chicago Cubs is another more recent example—he's been unable to throw to first base. He finds it hard to execute one of the simplest throws in baseball, from the pitcher's mound to first base, even reverting to bouncing throws to first base in an attempt to find some comfortability.

POSTGAME WRAP-UP

Understanding time and ego in the context of decision making will help you to stay centered when making a call, preventing unnecessary influence from past successes or failures. Whether a previous fourth-down gamble results in a first down or turnover on downs, with the right mindset you will be prepared to make the next decision . . . and to make the right decision.

The best judgments come by understanding what kinds of calls are in your comfort zone, learning zone, and anxiety zone, respectively, and then using your values to expand the comfort and learning zones, or reducing the decisions that put you into the anxiety zone. Achieve an even keel with the tools at your disposal—gratitude, empathy, accountability, and effective communication—to enable you to go from the anxiety zone back into the learning zone. This, in essence, will allow you to get out of your own way and keep you from tripping over the first-down markers behind you.

5

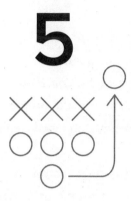

Being in the Game

PREGAME ANALYSIS

One of the most vital components of decision making revolves around your perspective of time. Are you focused on the decisions ahead of you, or are your thoughts directed elsewhere? Being focused on the game you're in, instead of the past or future, is essential for success. Pitchers who are thinking or obsessing about previous innings are less likely to strike out the batter they're currently facing. A team is unlikely to win the game they're playing today if they are focused on a future matchup. Don't get caught looking ahead! Persevering through lows, as well as maintaining composure through highs, comes from making today a focal point. Today is a day to make progress. We shouldn't worry about what has already happened or about what might happen in the future.

Maintaining a clear focus on today comes about when you learn to master a couple of different mental strategies. First, you have to understand how faith works. Most of us understand the importance of putting our faith in what we want in order to prepare us to achieve it. Fewer people understand the importance of not putting faith in the things that they do not want. Like a team that plays not to lose (and ends up losing), putting faith in something negative happening more often than not results in manifesting the exact situations we want to avoid.

Staying in the game also comes from your approach to goal setting. Learn to be consistent and persistent in the goals you chase, while also detaching your happiness from the outcome you seek. Telling yourself that you will be happy only after you achieve a certain thing will keep you focused on the future instead of inspiring you to grind in the present. Understand how to build momentum by first lowering the bar, then ratcheting up your efforts as you progress. Placing the right attention and intention on your goals, being persistent in the enjoyment of your pursuit of your potential, and continuing to hone the skills and knowledge to achieve are all essential. The decision to work toward your best self every day will keep you in the game—even if you face a tough loss or two along the way.

THE GAME IS ABOUT DEALING WITH HIGHS AND LOWS

After putting in a tremendous effort in high school, I was able to play football at Occidental College, both as a defensive back and a punt returner. The positions I played had many ups and downs. You are either the hero or the goat. There are very few times you hear the announcer say, "Oh, my gosh, unbelievable play from the center." Linemen are not really highlighted, unless they screw up, which is seemingly rare.

My football coach in college had a great saying to help me stay focused and in the present moment, he would continually remind us through the ups and the downs: "Just keep playing." Whenever I would get toasted for a touchdown (often enough), I would always have the chance to return the kickoff back for a touchdown the other way. In fact, one of the first things I did as a freshman was give up a big touchdown. My defensive coordinator had told me not to go for the interception, but I hadn't listened, instead seeing it tip off my fingers, with the other team bringing it down and scoring on a big play.

When I got back to the sideline, I was promptly screamed at by my defensive coordinator. He was so mean that he made me, an 18-year-old freshman, cry. He was so upset, he told the head coach not to put me back in to return the kick. But my head coach said, "No, let him return it." So there I was, standing and crying on the field, about to receive a kickoff. To everyone's surprise, I ended up returning it for a touchdown. Jubilant, I did a flip into the end zone, tossing the ball to the defensive coordinator on the sidelines, saying, "Money, money." That's the point at which the coach told me to just keep playing the game. He reminded me that the lows and highs will both pass. The important thing is to just keep playing.

In that instance, I learned a great lesson about the energy that you put into both business and life. If you put faith in the positives, you will get more positives. If you merely act in the hope of reducing the negatives, that's what you will receive. Warren Moon's career is a great example of this in action. He's lived with a majesty of calmness. He's QB Wan Kenobi. He approached the game with a sense of enjoyment, not trepidation. I've watched more Warren Moon film than I've watched Netflix content . . . and that's a lot. I've seen him win playoff games. I've seen him throw 527 yards against the number one defense at the time, the Kansas City Chiefs, and I've seen him lose a 32-point lead to the Buffalo Bills, missing out on a Super Bowl appearance.

The one thing that I know about Warren is that he still had this enjoyment of the pursuit of his potential. He was fighting it, but he didn't lie down on the field, crying, when they lost to the Buffalo Bills. And when he beat Kansas City, in that big game, a nice fist pump to celebrate is how he reacted. He got a little bit higher, but he wasn't wasting energy. He was in a majesty of calmness. I would've been breakdancing and doing backflips. But then I'm also not a Hall of Fame–caliber athlete.

You see athletes all the time whose emotions are way up or way down. Well, what happens with this approach is that whether you're way up or way down, you're wasting energy. You want to be in the consistent, persistent enjoyment of the pursuit of your potential. It's a whole different feeling to live in joy, to live *consistently* in happiness, understanding that you can be inspired without wasting energy. To live this way, you have to detach from outcomes.

Think about how many football players have said to themselves, "I'll be happy when I win the Super Bowl." Well, how many players actually have won a Super Bowl during their careers? Just a small fraction. But if they had instead enjoyed the consistent, persistent pursuit of their potential, their inspiration would have come from being in the game, putting their faith in their pursuit to be their highest self.

FAITH IS A TWO-WAY PLAYER

A lot of people think faith works in only one way. *I hope that this positive thing happens*, whether it's a specific desire or a broad one. I think it's a disruptive thought to think that faith works only in a positive direction. If you're not aware that you're putting faith in negative things, then you're not aware that you're attracting those negative things to yourself. When you put faith in what you *don't* have, that means you're not playing the game, and you're not in the present.

If you put faith in your fears, you manifest your fears. "I'm going to fumble this ball." "I'm so worried they're going to score a touchdown on me." "I'm worried that I won't be ready when my number is called." If you think these things, guess what happens? More often than not, your fears will come true. Think about it in terms of a relief pitcher. If you've got a great pitch that you rely on—take Mariano Rivera's cut fastball, for example—what makes more sense? Having faith in that cut fastball, or worrying about the other pitches that you *don't* have in your arsenal?

You may not always be aware that it's happening, but when you put faith in what you *don't* want, you're almost guaranteed to get what you don't want. It's a matter of perspective. The consistent, persistent enjoyment of the pursuit of your potential helps you work hard in the present not only to achieve your goals but also to be happy and fulfilled, whether you win the Super Bowl or not.

If you're happy, it doesn't matter what's going on with the game that you are playing. It doesn't matter how much money you have, what's going on in your life, or what other people consider good or bad. I've met paralyzed people who were much happier than the average person who has four working limbs. They're incredible, they're happy, they know what they want. And that's truly part of being in the game—knowing what your objectives are.

GO AFTER YOUR GOALS

After your overall objectives come subcategories—that is, subgoals of what you might want. I believe that to get what you want, you have to be consistent. I think consistency is even more important than persistence because consistency breeds persistence. Meaning, if you get in the habit of doing a particular thing every single day, quitting that habit is difficult. If I identify three things that I want in my life, subsets of being happy—goals such as improving my relationship with my mother, improving my health, and hiring someone for my media team—I know there are steps I need to take to achieve those goals. I then assign a minimum amount of time every day to those things.

So I assign a minimum amount of time each day to show my mother that I love and appreciate her. This is partly selfish, of course. I understand that if she doesn't feel loved, she's going to make me prove that I love and appreciate her, which takes up a different kind of time and energy. When it comes to my health, I know that if I'm not healthy, I won't be able to take care of the many things that are important in my life and business, without which I can't be happy. And knowing that I won't be satisfied until my media team has all of the assets necessary to excel, I need to hire one more person to fill out the team.

I spend a minimum of five minutes a day trying to fill out the media team. Why only five minutes? Because doing something just five minutes a day, every single day, is worth more than spending two hours on a Tuesday night with another team member trying to figure it out. Why do I believe that? Because of the exponential growth factor that consistency provides. If I do something every day, the first day I'll have some progress. If my starting point is at number 1, I'll be at some number greater than 1, whatever variable it is that I'm working on.

Day 2, you get the exponential improvement, with that number greater than 1 increased to the power of 2. You still get that exponential benefit on days 3, 4, 5, 6, and more, as long as you keep working on that subgoal every day. What happens to people is that somewhere along the line, they think that their inspiration and persistent attitude are enough to keep going—and eventually they forget.

Their momentum is gone, due to what I call the **zero effect**. That's why when people are trying to do things based on their perception of linear time—which is a man-made construct—they feel at the end of the month as if they have gotten no results despite relatively consistent effort. They put in effort at the beginning and at the end of a project or task, and they are often unsatisfied with the way that things turned out. Why do you get incremental results? You did this almost every day, for 28 days out of 30, but you zeroed out your progress two different times. The exponential growth factor and progress you can experience is reset each time you fail to work on that sub-goal. Even though we feel that we've worked the entire month, missing two days costs you the desired outcome.

> **ZERO EFFECT:** A negative impact on your progress associated with inconsistency. Without consistency and persistence, it is difficult to maintain your momentum toward your goals.
>
> X^1, then X^2, then X^3, until you miss a day, resulting in X^0, which equals 1.

Your thoughts, actions, and words dictate your reality. If we don't control those, working on our thought roster every day, then our focus on the present doesn't move from the conscious to the subconscious and, finally, the unconscious, where we don't have to think about it. The same holds true with all these other things, so with respect to being in the game and the importance of consistency, think about your objectives. Look at the great athletes like Tom Brady. They're the epitome of consistency. With all sports and in life, success is always a matter of consistency.

Phil Mickelson may not be one of the greatest athletes you've ever seen, but he's a darn good golfer who's been pretty consistent since he was 14 years old. It feels like he's won every single championship there is. OK, maybe he's not the greatest golfer of all time, but he's up there, and that's because he's so consistent. He's one of the most skilled players of all time because he's been playing golf consistently and practicing during much of his spare time.

Suppose I gave you the choice between spending six hours playing golf every Saturday or spending 30 minutes every day playing golf each week, and you chose to play golf six hours every Saturday. Come December 31 in that year, your game would be equal to or even worse than it was when you started. But not one golfer would be worse if she practiced 30 minutes a day, working on her driver, irons, putter, and short game. It's the energy of this consistency that is what leads to consistent improvement. And that's what you need to do to be in the game.

Consistency creates persistency. How can you do something every day and quit? These words don't even belong in the same sentence. I tell people, look, I just enjoy the consistent, persistent pursuit of my potential every day, whatever it may be that I'm doing—potential as a son when I call my mom, potential as a human being when I work to improve my health by working out, meditating, and eating right, and potential as a business leader when I spend time each day looking for the right new employee to add to the team. Your consistency creates persistence because if your habit is to do something every day, there's no way you're going to quit. In fact, the best piece of entrepreneurial advice that I give to people is this: stay in business.

The first thing I do every day when I wake up is think to myself, "What do I have to do today to make sure that I'm in business tomorrow?" Because if I'm in business tomorrow,

I know that I'm in the consistent, persistent pursuit of my potential. The day that you become inconsistent is the day you could go out of business. Why is Amazon growing while JCPenney and Toys R Us are struggling? I would tell you it's because they weren't in the game. They weren't consistently, persistently in the pursuit of their potential.

You can be born with the greatest talents and gifts, but if you're not persistent and consistent in the use of those skills, you cannot achieve your fullest potential. I promise you, there are plenty of people on the PGA golf tour who are more talented than Phil Mickelson, especially now that he's deep into his forties.

I think about the 2009 British Open when it comes to the role of persistence and consistency in success. One of my other favorite golfers, Tom Watson, nearly won the tournament at age 59, having won five times previously. He lost on the fourth playoff hole, unfortunately, but his success was the talk of the golf world for months. Watson lost by one stroke, and at that time, there was no way you could argue that Tom Watson was the best golfer on tour. However, when it comes to The Open tournament, he may turn out to be the most consistent, persistent golfer of all time. He's kind of like Phil Mickelson in that aspect. He might not be Jack Nicklaus or Tiger Woods, but due to his consistency, Tom Watson is regarded as one of the greatest golfers of all time, which is why even though he was inducted in the World Golf Hall of Fame in 1988, he was able to compete with the PGA Tour "young bucks" and dominate the Senior Tour, with 14 wins on the Champions Tour, including six senior majors.

DETACH HAPPINESS FROM ACHIEVEMENT: GLORIFY THE PURSUIT, NOT THE GOAL

The perspective of achieving your goal, no matter how much effort it takes to reach it, will not make you happy. Michael Jordan said, "Winning isn't always championships."[1] Attaching your goals to happiness is what leads to unhappiness. So many people, including me, grow up believing that an achievement will automatically mean happiness:

> "Gosh, when I graduate from high school, I'm going to be so happy."
> "Oh, when I get married, I'll be so happy."
> "When I have kids, I'm going to be so happy."
> "When I make my first million dollars, I'm going to be so happy."

Guess what never comes? Your happiness. In fact, the time in my life that I had the most was also the emptiest I've ever felt. I remember building my dream home, lying in bed, and thinking to myself, "Oh, shit." And the reason was I had no consistent, persistent pursuit of anything except monetary gain. Eventually, I figured some of it out. I would say, "Don't worry how you get there. The Universe has something even bigger in store for you, but you have to pursue what you want." This is how I take things from possibility, to probability, to perspective.

This choice, choosing to detach from an outcome, can

seem extremely conflictual, and it is hard for people to understand. One of the common questions I get is this: "How do you have goals yet remain detached from an outcome?" The truth is, I'm very driven toward the goals I set. As I discussed in the previous chapter, I try to take my ego and time, two driving factors for many, out of my goal setting.

What I do is this: I set a goal, and at the same time, I detach my happiness from the goal. I do not create an immediate plan to get to my goal. My plan, when I start out, is simply to provide value toward that overall goal every single day. I literally do an assessment each day to determine the amount of effort I've put forth and whether I'm receiving incremental or exponential results as I proceed. There's no set plan for how I'm going to "get to the Super Bowl." All I know is that if I wake up every day looking to provide value to 10 people the Universe puts in front of me, while also making sure that I continue to spend at least some minimum amount of time and energy working toward my subgoals, the value I give will yield consistent results.

Approach every situation contemplating how much value you can provide, and you will get value in return. Just like practice squad players or minor leaguers who aren't quite where they want to be in their career, putting in effort and providing value to those around you will lead you to needed opportunities in the future.

At the same time as you're chasing your goals, you must understand that there is no defined "finish line." That's why it can be helpful to view the goals as the yard markers on a football field with no defined end zone. You might not know exactly where you are in relation to your goals, but paying attention to the yard markers as you progress can empower you to be confident in your pursuit of a touchdown.

When raising money for my charity, the Unstoppable Foundation, I desire to raise more than $1 million, knowing that exceeding that number would enable the organization to launch myriad different projects. It has upset me, though, when people have said things like, "Oh, you're raising $1 million for Unstoppable." No, I have never said that. That's not me. I'm raising *more* than a $1 million. That $1 million number is just a marker that I want to pass along my journey.

Limiting beliefs prevent you from maintaining a proper perspective. For example, as previously discussed, I used to think, when I was just five years old, that if I made $1 million, I would never have to work again and that was the most money that I would ever need. Now that idea is laughable, especially having lost millions upon millions of dollars in the 2008 real estate crash.

So, go ahead and set markers, but don't put an attachment in the end to what you want. You're limiting yourself by taking that approach, I promise you. Whatever it is that you want, there's always something bigger and better, and over your lifetime, as you improve your awareness, you will be able to see it. As long as you avoid the traps of time and ego and you are consistent and persistent in pursuing what you want, you will stay in the game.

If you want to achieve your goals, start by setting your mind on what you want, and make it your marker. Identify what skills, knowledge, and desires are necessary to achieve that, and choose to prioritize acquiring them in your life. Make it one of your three subgoals to ensure that you are constantly chasing those skills, knowledge, or desires. Come up with a plan for how to provide value as you progress. Don't simply plan to get to the outcome. Use your desires to aid in building the skills, knowledge, and necessary inspiration to attract what you want. Allow things to happen by detaching from outcomes. When you can take what you think about and become inspired, it will become another mathematical advantage called a *probability*. So, you get *possibility* when you think about a goal, and *probability* when you're inspired by it.

I used to say there's only one thing that stands in your way from allowing your goal to be your reality or allowing it to be your perspective, and that's you. But I will say there are two things incorporated in you, two things that stop you from allowing things to happen. One is time, which is a human-made construct, and the other is ego, which causes feelings like the need to be right, the need to be offended, the need to be separate, the need to be in fear, or the need to be superior. When you get out of your own way, detach your happiness from your goals, and allow something to happen, the outcome you are seeking will come faster and more accurately than you can imagine. If you want to be a professional athlete, for example, you must focus on it every day. Take concrete steps to make it your reality. Think about the skills, the knowledge, and the desire to be a professional athlete, and that's the first step for you to acquire it.

I was talking to one of my coaching clients the other day, a professional basketball player who stands five-feet-two, when I had a realization. After learning about his journey and the obstacles he conquered on the way, I said, "You've helped me realize that I was living below the line and not being accountable. For years I've told people my story about how I wanted to be a professional football player, and how the 'Nigerian Nightmare' Christian Okoye ran me over in college, which made me decide I was too small to be a professional football player."

I think the truth that I realize now is that I didn't have the skills, the knowledge, or the desire that it took to make that goal a reality. It had nothing to do with my size because if it had, then there would be no five-foot-seven professional football players in the NFL. The truth is that those players do exist, and there have even been players like Trindon Holliday who checked in at five-feet-five. Somewhere along the line, we tend to lie to ourselves, often due to our perception of ego or time, and we make excuses, saying, "Well, this is why I didn't manifest what I dreamed of." When people say your dreams are impossible, think about what Henry Ford said: "Whether you think you can, or you think you can't—you're right."[2] Get out of your own way, identify the time and the ego issues you're facing, and allow the things to happen.

Think about how many times we say to ourselves, "It's too late. I can't do that." We think it's too late to do something different, like change professions. Countless entrepreneurs have proven that idea false. Ray Kroc sold milkshake machines until learning about the McDonald brothers' burgeoning businesses at age 51.[3] Orville Redenbacher was 63 before he got his big break, landing his namesake popcorn into a Marshall Field's department store.[4] If someone asks you how old you are, tell them you're timeless. Don't let time get in your way. There's always tomorrow, whether you're 20, 30, 40, or 50. Or even 60, 70, 80, or 90. Why should time be in your way? And then, of course, we all know our ego can put us in our own way, creating untrue perceptions in its attempts to safeguard us, while also obscuring the truth.

INTENTION VERSUS ATTENTION

When you set the priorities for what you want, you need to have **intention**—the mindset that pushes you toward what you want. When living with a consistent, persistent pursuit of your potential, I believe you can have the best intentions, but those intentions will not always be able to carry you through to success if you don't pay enough **attention** to how closely your actions are aligned with your core values.

> **INTENTION:** A drive or desire to succeed that needs to be combined with consistent attention in order to achieve desired results.
>
> **ATTENTION:** The amount of energy or care directed to a task, action, goal, or core value.

I would tell someone that is not aligned with gratitude, empathy, accountability, and effective communication, I wished he were making those mistakes on purpose, because if they were doing it on purpose, it would be much easier just to get rid of them. Unfortunately, most people make mistakes with good intent, which means that in order to fix the mistake, it requires much more attention and work to re-engineer their actions, allowing them to align with the four core values. As silly as it sounds, as an efficient leader, I wish more people would make intentional mistakes. It would make my job a lot easier.

When my favorite employee of all time screwed up, I said, "I wish you were doing this intentionally because then I could just fire you, but I love you because you have the best intentions." What was he missing? Well, chances are you've seen it in every sport. Players blame their football coach for their own shortcomings. Inexperienced business professionals (as well as experienced ones) may have the best intentions, but what they don't have breaks my heart: attention—which is *focus*.

Attention allows you to take your intention, that is, the possibility, and put focus to it. Clarity, balance, and focus. Focus brings attention and inspiration—and inspiration is timeless. When you're inspired, there is no time. Have you ever watched a movie that was very inspirational? You say, "Whoa. That was two and a half hours?" And have you ever seen the cinematic disaster that is *Water World*? Watching that movie feels like it takes *two and a half weeks*. The difference was that we were emotionally involved and invested in those inspirational TV shows, movies, podcasts, and speeches. They're timeless.

Practice does not make perfect. What it does is enable us to pursue our best self, rooted in strong values and inspiration. Practice only pursues perfection. It never gets there. If that old saying were really true, there would be billions of perfect people out there. Rather, it's a deliberate practice with intention and attention that allows you to steadily progress with whatever skills you're looking to improve. Utilize the power of intention every day to gain the skills you need to effect change in your life. Taking stock of the reasons that you want to make the change is a great place to start, then look to your intentions and realize where you can improve. You need to give your skills your attention and focus every single day to yield exponential growth results.

Recent Pro Football Hall of Fame inductee Ray Lewis is a perfect example of what happens when you are consistent and persistent in your pursuit of what you desire. Ray wanted to play college football more than anything. He even left his mother, the person he cared most about in the entire world, in order to put himself in the position to play high school football. And even though he was an athlete who put his heart and soul into the game, his entire high school career came and went without an offer to go to college . . . that was until four days before National Signing Day his senior year.

Because he had worked so hard for his goals, honed his skills, accrued knowledge, and showed immense desire, his efforts were eventually recognized by the University of Miami. The school's coaching staff saw him play his last high school game by coincidence, when they had come to watch the number one recruit in the country play against Ray's school. After seeing him play, the coaches decided to offer Ray a scholarship after another linebacker in their recruiting class was injured. Ray made the most of his opportunity, and it led him to have one of the more successful careers in NFL history. How often does that happen to those who are not consistent and persistent? Not very often.

I knew a kid, a talented teenage baseball player, who ended up in an uncomfortable situation involving what his family deemed "politics" on his traveling baseball team. The perception was that for whatever reason, other kids were jealous of him, and he ended up not getting invited back to play on the team after the first season. He felt that his chances of getting recruited, and eventually drafted, were over, but nevertheless was consistent and persistent in the pursuit of his potential.

A lot of us who've participated in sports have experienced similar "not fair" situations: "I should be starting." "I should have made that team." "I deserve a shot." During my sports career, I was usually the last guy when I joined a team that they thought would make the team, let alone play, which was the best lesson in my life because I was consistent and persistent despite that.

Well, this young man I knew was consistent and persistent, so he went to the batting cages all the time that he would have been playing with that traveling squad. He practiced on his own because he hadn't made the team. Lo and behold, one day when he was practicing, a scout noticed him, a scout who was there to watch the travel team that was playing on the field next to the cage. As it happened, that scout looked over and saw this kid swinging and taking cut after cut. The two started talking, and the scout ended up giving him a tryout, and that young man eventually ended up playing in the major leagues.

You've got to be consistent and persistent, despite the limiting beliefs of others, because if you do it every day, you'll never quit.

RAISE YOUR GAME BY LOWERING THE BAR

In terms of being consistent, one strategy that I have found to be helpful is lowering the bar. I know everybody else in the world will implore you to raise the bar. However, staying in the game allows us to achieve more than even we can conceive, and to do so, you need to try to lower the bar.

Why? What does that mean? What stops us from pursuing what we want, a lot of times, is that the bar seems too high, due to lofty goals that seem so far away or difficult to achieve. So, I say lower the bar because 2 minutes a day is worth more than 30 minutes a week. If you want to build momentum, you don't have to tell yourself, "I'm going to do this for an hour a day." Why? Once again, you're messing with time, you're messing with the Universe, and you're messing with your ego.

Lower the bar. Tell yourself, "I'm going to give this task

a minute. A minimum of a minute," Why? It's a marker. It's a minimum of a minute, once per day, every day. Because when you think about doing that task, there's no burden to it because you lowered the bar.

That was the way I started working out when I was nearly 50 pounds heavier than I am right now. I was tired of the way that I presented on stage, often telling myself and my wife, each time I looked in the mirror, "Oh, I've got to work out." But I didn't want to go to the gym. It seemed like a huge task. So, I set about setting low bars. "Tomorrow, I'm going to put my tennis shoes on." That's what I set out to do to start. "At a minimum, I'm going to put my tennis shoes on tomorrow." I set the bar that low to make it easy for me to start getting some momentum toward my true goal.

That night I laid the shoes out, laid them right in the middle of my closet. The next morning, I woke up at my normal time, 4 a.m., and I meditated. Then I looked at the shoes, and I said, "All right." I put on my socks, and I put on my shoes. And then I kept going. I put on my shorts, and I put on a t-shirt. Grabbed my keys. "You know what? I'm just going to go to the gym and check out what they have. Tomorrow, maybe I'll do something."

Got to the gym. I looked, and there was the elliptical trainer. "You know what? I'll get on for 15 minutes." I jumped on the machine. Low-tension resistance. I started at two or three. Fifteen minutes after I started, the low-tension setting was too easy. Four, five, six, seven, eight, right? Ten. That was enough.

I got through 30 minutes. I felt like I was going to have a heart attack, but I did it. I went home, and I felt better.

The next day, I put on my whole outfit. I said, "I'm just going to put my outfit on today." I just promised myself consistently. "That's all I'm going to do today. I'm going to make sure I put on the stuff to wear to go to the gym."

Once again, I put it on, the keys were right there, I went to the gym, and boom: another 30 minutes. I raised the bar as I progressed, of course, but that was not the strategy I used to get my momentum going.

Lower the bar. Make it feel like there's no resistance because that resistance is existing in what you think, say, and do. If you don't think this is true, then why is it that, when you start to work out and you get into the groove, you feel like you're missing something when you're not working out? You also have to be aware enough to hold yourself back some days and say, "I'm not going to put on my workout gear because actually my body needs a rest." That's true with every single thing in your life.

POSTGAME WRAP-UP

Being in the game empowers you to enjoy the consistent, persistent pursuit of your potential. This mindset encourages you to keep playing, through the tough times as well as the winning streaks, while remaining focused on the next call you have to make.

Combining a positive intention with faith in what you want, instead of what you don't want, will help you maintain your focus as well as your momentum.

Goal setting is, of course, essential to making progress, which is why taking the right approach to those goals is a fundamental part of decision making. Choose to be consistent and persistent in the way that you go after what you want. Dedicate a minimum amount of attention to your goals every single day. Build momentum toward your goals, and pay attention to the yard markers along the way, by first starting with a lower bar.

Once you understand how to exceed your own initial expectations, and you continually raise those expectations, you will have a clearer path to your desires as long as you can detach your happiness from achievement and instead focus on enjoying the steps you take along the way.

With persistence and practice, staying attuned to the present and being in the game will come naturally, as will achieving your goals and appreciating the game you played to get there.

6

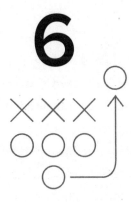

The Offense and Defense of Branding

PREGAME ANALYSIS

When building a personal or corporate brand, you need to understand when to be aggressive and when to be defensive. Finding the right balance of offense and defense is essential when determining how best to brand an individual, group, or company. And to find a brand message that reverberates in your target market, you must first understand the difference between a brand's frequency and its identity.

A *brand frequency* is a value proposition and emotional connection that is aligned with your target market or demographic, while a *brand identity* is the perception of your brand, combined with features and benefits associated with a brand's or organization's assets.

In football terms, a frequency is a lot like the systems that are in place for the offense or defense, something that varies greatly from team to team and organization to organization. College football fans, for example, know that Washington State Head Coach Mike Leach is one of the biggest advocates of the Air Raid Offense, an offense designed around shotgun formations and (predominately) four wide receiver sets, often run without a huddle.

Learn to understand your brand's frequency, as well as how to adapt that frequency when communicating with your audience. Ensuring that your brand is aligned with the needs and desires of others is aided by being able to create *asks* and *attracts* that blend emotion and logic, which is important because people tend to buy on emotion for reasons that feel internally logical. People will have some sort of emotional connection to a brand company, product, or service, and then they search their minds for a logical reason to justify taking action.

Sports memorabilia is a perfect example of this. An official MLB baseball, which costs $22.99, will be worth hundreds or thousands if it is signed by an athlete. After the initial urge to buy a signed ball, fans will justify the reasons to buy it—whether they are fans of the player whose signature graces the ball, it reminds them of a particular moment in their fanhood, or they are simply speculating on its future value.

Finding a way to tap into emotions like nostalgia, when appropriate, can help elevate a brand in the minds of others, as long as your brand's messaging is communicated with authenticity and consistency. How well you get your brand's point across depends largely on the content you provide. You can also maximize the impact of your ideas by choosing the right points of access and mediums to share those ideas. In this chapter, you will learn not only how to formulate a brand, both personal and professional, but also how to use emotion and strong values to build a wealth of interest in that brand, interest which you can leverage for success.

FINDING A FREQUENCY

The first step of branding something is to find its frequency. What does that mean, "to find your brand's frequency"? Whether it's building a brand that is a person, a place, a thing, a product, or a service, it's essential to find out what the "woo-woo" person in me describes as a "vibration"—in other words, an emotional appeal meant to reverberate with your target audience or market.

A frequency can best be described by talking about it in terms of radio stations. If we want sports talk radio, we turn to a specific channel. If we want rock 'n' roll, we'll find a station whose music (and employees) have that vibe. If we want cool jazz, that's a whole 'nother frequency. Only the people who are tied into that frequency will seek out or hear that radio station. The same thing holds true about branding.

You want a brand that rings true to your audience, something aligned with their beliefs, desires, or aspirations. You also want to find a frequency that enough people listen to, right? To connect to others and take your message, product, service, or solution mainstream to the biggest audience, you first need to fully understand who you are, what you're selling, how you're selling it, and the value that it brings to others. You need to understand how your frequency, or that of your product, resonates with others and attracts them to the brand that you're trying to establish.

Unfortunately, many people tend to confuse the brand with their own identity, which is your perception of your own frequency. Your identity is who you are. Your brand is the vehicle that empowers you to connect with others. And, more often than not, humans desire to connect emotionally. So, the frequency of human beings relative to their products, services, and solutions is an emotional connection.

Identity comes from your perception, while the brand comes from outside perspectives—in other words, other people's perspectives. This is why we want to build our brand from the foundation of a frequency instead of an identity. To find your frequency, or the frequency of a brand, you need to take stock in what it *is*—not what others tell you it is or what they perceive it to be. So many times in life, we try to listen to other people to find our own frequency. The optimal approach is actually the exact opposite. By finding our own frequency of products, services, or solutions, we can attract the widest audience and access the people the brand should address.

When you're looking at your frequency and looking within your own ideas, you have to find that frequency yourself, then test it out. Strong brands are built by those who understand that "I am," instead of those who listen to others who say, "You are" or "You aren't." The people who live in the realm of "You are" have trouble finding a frequency, and I see it all the time with products, solutions, and services.

People don't know the frequency of the solution they're providing, just as many of us don't know the frequency of ourselves. When individuals don't know the frequency of what they're selling, they tend to listen to other people and make misguided, disingenuous, or misinformed decisions.

I see it with my media team members who help out with my brand building on Instagram. We get thousands of positive comments on a regular basis, and then one commenter will say something negative, and our team will panic. They'll say, "Oh, we've got to change this." My first reaction is to ask them why we need to make changes if there is only one person who is not at our frequency. With billions of people in the world, all you need for success is to find a miniscule percentage whose values and goals are aligned with your brand.

When talking about emotional connections in sports, one term tends to stick out in my mind: *rivalry*. The biggest rivals tend to have differing frequencies, something you can see in the way that teams and organizations brand themselves.

The Boston Red Sox and New York Yankees are shining examples of branding a specific frequency and adapting that frequency based on current circumstances. For the longest time, the Red Sox branded themselves as underdogs with a rich history, perpetually competing as David and Goliath against their championship-laden counterparts. The Yankees, of course, branded themselves as the winningest organization in sports history, with an unmatched list of all-time greats who have worn the storied Yankee pinstripes. Now, the Red Sox, who since 2004 have had more success in the playoffs and World Series games they've played in, are forced to adapt. The Red Sox are now in the big-spender role, with their increased payroll numbers leading to World Series Championships in 2013 and 2018. This reversal of fortunes means that the Red Sox can no longer carry a frequency that they are second fiddle to the Yankees. They must tap into the emotions of winning, while also staying on message regarding the rich history of the club.

You're asking for trouble, limiting yourself and your brand, when you start listening to what others say that you are. You've got to know your frequency and believe in it. Without a steadfast belief, you will also miss the confidence that comes along with a strong brand and frequency. Does that mean you can't adjust your frequency? Of course not! If I'm putting out a frequency for a youth sports league and all I'm attracting to my brand are 70-year-old men, I want to consider changing the frequency and content that I put out because my current approach is not going to be profitable. It may be passion with a purpose, but it won't yield profitability.

The root of your frequency comes from your core beliefs and values. Think about the beliefs you had when you were born. You held no beliefs whatsoever when you were born, so where did they originate from? Your environment. They came from the people and ideas that surrounded you and later that you surrounded yourself with, which is where all of your beliefs come from. Those beliefs came from a frequency that you surrounded yourself with, and those frequencies can be moved, shifted, adjusted, grown, and elevated—but this occurs only when you know your own truth. That is why you must be secure in who you are, what your product is, what your values are, and what you (or your brand) stand for.

When you take the time to evaluate the reasons people use a product or service, as well as the impacts or capabilities that it has, then you'll be able to emotionally connect or communicate to others what that brand is. Once you have a frequency, you can test the frequency through your social media. You can post a message or piece of content and see what it attracts. And if it starts attracting what you want in terms of engagement, hits, click-throughs, comments, or some other measurable way, you can post more content along the same lines.

With the pervasiveness of the Internet, with a few clicks of a button you can buy more ads to that content (or you can buy ads for other brand-aligned content with similar emotional appeals or messaging), and you can thus continue to build that brand around consistent messages, themes, and values. In fact, a major part of the process is refining and adjusting the frequency you give off. Then we use the ask and attract methodology to perpetuate and grow that brand.

SCORING BRANDING POINTS
WITH ASK AND ATTRACT

On the offensive side of branding, the first step is to find your frequency. It is only when you know all of the assets that you have that you are able to defend that brand. The second step comes when you learn to ask and attract. That's an aggressive approach of building a brand. In fact, I would say that's the "offensive approach." An organization, business, or person on the offensive seeks to grow the brand simply by asking for and attracting what they want. And when you hold true to your frequency and grow that frequency, evolve that frequency, you'll keep attracting.

Now, what is ask and attract? Let's start with making an **ask**. If you have yourself as a product, service, or solution or if you have an existing product, service, or solution, and you've found the frequency of that brand, then you need to ask people if they would like you to utilize it. If they wouldn't like it, it's not at their frequency, then you need to improve your statistical success by asking a second question: "Do you know anyone who might like it?" Those are the only two asks that you could have: "Do you want it?" or "Do you know somebody else who might want it?"

> **ASK:** A piece of information or content with a specifically designed ask built in for the target market that will inspire them to take action.

> **ATTRACT:** A piece of information or content with no clear ask but that instead has the goal of drawing the target audience's attention to a brand or inspires them to take some action, whether defined or undefined.

One of my favorite people on earth is not the most famous football player of all time. He might be described as a journeyman, having played 11 years, including for the San Diego Chargers, New Orleans Saints, and Minnesota Vikings. He's actually a gentleman who's worked for me three times, named Vencie Glenn. My favorite thing about Vencie Glenn is that he has lived by his one motto: "You don't get unless you ask." Vince survived in the NFL *and* in business because he asked for something when he needed it. It is amazing that so many of us do so much for others but ask for so little. We have no problem when people ask us for something, but we're just afraid to ask for something for ourselves. Failing to ask, "Do you know somebody else who can help me?" is mathematically limiting ourselves. It would be as if we were asking only one person for help.

In general, there are four basic ways to ask: in person, over the phone, and via email or social media. Statistically, you stand a better chance for success if you have some sort of strategic ask in almost everything that you do, no matter the medium. Think about it mathematically: if you make one additional ask per day and convert at around 10 percent, then you will have three people each month providing you with benefits that you'd have missed otherwise.

Now there's a whole 'nother side of branding beyond asks. There are also what I call "attracts." Attracts take a little bit more work to get down pat. These are messages designed to attract what we want. To use an attract efficiently, we put out a frequency that attracts people to gain their interest.

Circling back to the Red Sox example, an attract could be as simple as a piece of digital content showing Sox fans celebrating their newest World Series win with their family, combined with a message related to a family ticket promotion. With that content, the team has connected emotionally to their fans, tapping into the emotions and collective belief that comes with a championship team. Because people buy on emotion for logical reasons, their target market can't help but consider buying tickets for the upcoming year, with the anticipation that there will be more to celebrate in the future. There is a strong emotional pull, having just experienced a winning season, followed by all sorts of potential logical reasons to repurchase, such as a tangible reminder of the benefits of a previous season ticket purchase or the knowledge that failure to renew could mean going back on a wait list for future seasons.

There are all kinds of emotional things that have a value that money cannot buy, that compel you to move forward. That's branding and that's attraction. So, you can ask in person, in email, on the phone, or on social media, or you can attract.

The Red Sox example is a perfect reminder that frequency

is based on emotional response. Branding is an emotional frequency, not an identity associated with features. What happens when you go on the offense in branding, when you do it every day without quitting, and when you enjoy the pursuit of building a brand, is you can instill your objectives with inspiration because most people love to connect to other people emotionally.

When you stick to your frequency, connect to people emotionally, and actually make it a habit to ask and attract, a brand can go from the offensive, where we have to ask, to the defensive, where we can slow down and take time to deal with things such as a wait list for your product, service, or solution. Eventually, you'll have a frequency which vibrates at a speed that attracts so many people you won't be able to handle the business. You'll have a brand so powerful that people will sleep outside for two days on the street to buy tickets to an event or to get the next version of your phone.

STAGE THEORY: BRAND MESSAGING WITH CONSISTENCY AND AUTHENTICITY

No matter what your frequency is, your messaging needs to have two things: authenticity, which is emotion-based, and consistency. You need to be asking and attracting every day. When you are not authentic, your frequency will either connect you to the wrong people, or it won't connect you at all.

When you are inconsistent with a message or brand, either in the way you deliver a message or by delivering it at inconsistent intervals, you'll find it difficult to capture and keep an audience, no matter what content you're putting out.

When I met with Gary Vaynerchuk, I was one of the few people ever to ask him directly what I wanted, without hesitation or beating around the bush. I made a direct ask: "Gary, I want more engaged followers on social media."

He grabbed my phone, took a look at my Instagram profile, and said, "Oh, yeah, no problem. You don't put enough content up. You're doing all the right things, your ideas are amazing, but the consistency is not there. You're inconsistent, Dave."

After that, we turned a switch of consistency on in the brand. We went from being on the verge of defensive, to *overwhelmingly* defensive, with more interest in our brand than ever before.

Now, if you're asking and attracting via in-person, phone, email, and social media contacts, there are certain components that can accelerate or provide you exponentially better results, especially the idea itself. Gatorade, for example, has long worked to align the Gatorade brand with another "G": greatness. When the company came out with its initial G commercials, many wondered what the hell that G stood for. To answer that, Gatorade chose to tie in frequencies of transcendent athletes such as Muhammad Ali and Michael Jordan. What was the frequency that the company was attaching to the G? Greatest of all time. Gatorade created a branded channel to connect you to an emotion with no clear product, service, or solution to be bought. It was only later that the company's messaging shared the logical reasons to purchase its products—a new formula, better hydration, improved performance, or something else. They dosed you up with the world's greatest, and when you felt it, then they put a product behind it.

This type of branding is likely what inspired Gatorade to then amplify the NBA's D-League brand. Realizing that there was such great alignment with their products, consumers, and the game of basketball, Gatorade took the opportunity to create a lifestyle brand that was beyond just a recovery drink. They took the audience of the D-League and transitioned them to align with Gatorade, simply by changing a letter in an already established brand, and the D-League became the NBA G League.

BRANDING WITH THE STAGE THEORY

Establishing a brand can be done most efficiently in three stages in what I call the *stage theory*.

> **STAGE THEORY:** Branding yourself, a company, product, or service in a way that amplifies and perpetuates your messages, exposing those messages to wider and wider audiences over time.

In stage 1, you create or capture some kind of content with a frequency. What does that mean? It connects an emotion, such as curiosity or nostalgia, to a brand and its message. Every piece of content, not just features or benefits, can be utilized if you attach it to an emotion, not an identity.

In stage 2, you provide access to your message. Access is how people experience the information. Remember, it's valuable information no matter if you have 10, 10 million, or 10 billion people to share that content with. Once you know your audience, then you can market the products, services, and solutions to that emotional frequency. If I knew that 50 percent of my audience cared about the Red Sox and Yankees' rivalry, for example, I would come up with some sort of content that played off of the emotions associated with the two teams.

Stage 3 is about choosing the medium: TV versus social media, in person versus email, email versus phone, phone versus the variety of different things on social media. The mediums are where your messages come across to your audience, and choosing the right medium is essential in making the best emotional connections. To further your brand, you need to know the frequency of these platforms and how to get emotion across in each of them. Then you need to test the audience in an evolutionary way to determine what content attracts which people. Look at the access you're giving to content, and what medium you provide that content on. When communicating with others to build a brand, it is important to understand these three components of distribution. The content is what others experience. The access is how they experience it. The medium is where they experience it.

Failure to choose the right content, access, and mediums limits your reach and the impact of your message, even if you're at the right frequency. If you try to put a sports talk radio show's frequency into a book, for example, it doesn't work. The medium won't get across the same emotions that people experience when listening to that show. When you capture, amplify, and perpetuate the frequency through your messaging, whether in person or via email, phone, social media, or some other platform, the different mediums all work together to build a harmonious brand.

Once you get a following, people who enjoy your content in whatever way you decide to deliver it, capture it, amplify it, and perpetuate it, along with the right content, access, and mediums, then you have to share your value through the other mediums. You can build an audience in one place and find your frequency, and then you can adapt that messaging to other points of access and different mediums with different types of content.

You've got to make sure your message is aligned with your business and your personal audience where you're addressing these people. Why is this important? Today's technology allows us to connect with more consumers than ever before. But focusing on digital-only content and branding is a huge mistake. Certainly you have to have traditional content to amplify onto the digital platforms, but I still say there's value in having a full-page ad in *Entrepreneur* magazine. For one thing, there's a certain frequency of people who read magazines, right? So, a full-page ad in *Entrepreneur* magazine has its value, but it gains exponential value when you can incorporate it into a digital video.

I used to weigh the worth of my speeches by how many people attended. What really amazes me now with the stage theory is that no matter where I speak, as long as the stage looks cool and the topic provides value, it doesn't matter how many people are there in person at that event because I can amplify the message across various media. It's one thing to put your message on traditional billboards in a stadium. It's another thing to incorporate the message on those billboards onto a tailgate sign and into the hospitality and the sideline pieces of gameday promotion. Instead of only attendees or viewers of the game seeing that message, by sharing it on other mediums, with different points of access, you amplify that message across a much broader audience.

Understand that the whole ecosystem of the traditional stage is . . . well, traditional. I don't care where you present it. I believe the traditional branding is on the stage, and the digital realm is where the amplification and the perpetuation of your message occur. So, you capture the content from whatever stage you are on and amplify it, and you can create a frequency and a reach like no other.

There's never been a better opportunity in your life to brand something, even on the playing field with big brands. You need to combine digital and traditional. It's important for you to learn how to promote your brand across multiple mediums and make sure to focus on the metrics of each of the audience. That's why all the data, the testing, and everything else about this approach is so important.

THE SUBTLETIES OF BRANDING

There are subtleties now in branding that will affect your success. One little tweak can make all the difference. And to be fair, it's always been that way. Brian Smith, founder of UGG Boots, is a good friend of mine. Brian was on the verge of going bankrupt. He brought over common Australian surf boots, and he hired surfers to wear them with no real results. Then he started hiring girls in bikinis to wear them while watching the surfers. That change resulted in improved awareness and sales. Then Oprah listed his boots as one of her top 10 Christmas gifts, and it took his company through the roof, and then he sold it to Deckers.

Those are the subtleties of success. For UGG Boots, one little tweak got the attention. It was a different frequency but the same product. Brian knew the product was good. It had all the features and benefits surfing boots should have. In all three places where surfing is part of the culture—Southern California, Australia, and Hawaii—people loved these boots, before and after surfing. But Brian knew there was a huge demand beyond that market. So, what did he do? He switched the brand's frequency into one of comfort, and he put a renewed focus on those who were the most emotionally attached to their shoes.

MAKING THE MOST OF BRANDING OPPORTUNITIES

Branding can be found in something as simple as an email signature. There are two main purposes to my signature, the first being to raise curiosity. I used to put "unconditionally" at the bottom of my emails because I wanted people to ask what that meant. It had a dual meaning: that I wanted to live or pursue my potential, which was to live without judgment or conditions, which meant unconditionally.

I used to have one of those long signatures, with the second purpose being to extol all of my accomplishments in an effort to brand myself as a multifaceted expert. It was only after realizing my frustration with similarly long signatures from others that I changed it to *res ipsa loquitur*, which is Latin for "that which speaks for itself." That message is a higher vibration, one that speaks for itself. If you don't know me, maybe if you're curious, you should go find out. Go find out what I've done. And if you're at my frequency, come join me.

Sports media firebrand and founder of *Barstool Sports*, Dave Portnoy built his brand on one thing: David and Goliath emotion. He took on the NFL, cannibalizing a humongous audience of the most popular sport while taking on not only the commissioner but the league, as well. He built a brand on that emotion, David and Goliath, us versus them, and that's the *Barstool Sports* frequency, all based on emotional appeal and the camaraderie of those who are aligned with that feeling. Is *Barstool Sports* content any better than anybody else's? No. But it has its own unique frequency. It has the same features and benefits of every other sports content provider that's out there, but the *Barstool Sports* writers have their own "locker room" frequency, like a fraternity of sports misfits. They've got sarcasm, humor, and one-bite pizza reviews, all staying with a message that's "us against them."

POSTGAME WRAP-UP

Branding yourself or your company is a factor of the emotional connection you make with a target market, whether in person, on the phone, or via email or social media, or some other medium of access. By building a brand every day, consistently, persistently, and with an authentic message, your frequency will resonate among those you desire to connect with.

Remember that connecting emotionally, using the stage theory, and capturing, amplifying, and perpetuating the right content with the right points of access and mediums are what will help you brand your message so that people can better understand the value you provide.

At the same time, the prevalence of the Internet places additional importance on understanding the subtleties of success. You must be able to adapt the emotional connection you establish via one means of contact across different mediums, whether they are traditional or digital.

By clearly understanding the information you desire to get across, the refined frequency of that information, and how that message will resonate with your target market, you can brand any opportunity that comes your way efficiently and effectively.

7

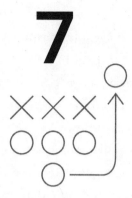

The Offense and Defense of Marketing

PREGAME ANALYSIS

When building a brand, you must learn to align with your core audience in order to market that brand most effectively. The question that this chapter is going to answer is, how do you find a combination of push and pull marketing (or ask and attract marketing) that best fits your products or services?

I like to tell people to position themselves and their products or services to make a lot of money, help a lot of people, and have a lot of fun, and to do that by understanding the desires of the market, as well as the values that the people you are targeting hold dear.

Not only do you need to learn to get aligned with your target market *before* launching your marketing efforts, but you also must have a complete grasp of the value you hold. Knowing your value, and how that value compares to competitors in the market, will empower you to make yourself equal to your competition. This, even though it might seem counterintuitive, is the first step in differentiating yourself from others.

Once you have a true understanding of the similarities between you and your competition, you can then make yourself different, and that difference will become an essential component in all of your marketing efforts. Simply perceiving these similarities and differences does nothing to market your business. You need to get off your ass, take action, and always be ready to make adjustments to your marketing plan. It's all about offense and defense, push and pull.

Whether you are creating marketing materials to push your consumers to take action or pull them closer to your brand and its message, you must be strategic in the ways that you connect to others. When you understand the best ways to compel your audience, including utilizing **bug lights** to drive traffic, then it is time to take advantage of the attention you've gained making the right asks.

> **BUG LIGHT:** A marketing asset that helps attract your target market buyers and inspires them to take action.

There is no "trick play" to stimulate interest with your marketing efforts. Having confidence and belief in the value you offer is key. If you're confident in what you're pitching and you truly believe in what you're marketing, then you will have a deep connection to your brand, product, service, and self, and ultimately to your target market.

THE AAA STRATEGY: ALIGNMENT, ACTION, ADJUSTMENT

The first thing you need to do in marketing is connect emotionally. People use logic to justify their emotional reasons to take action. Emotion in any message is energy in motion. It's the key to connecting to other people and realizing oneness, and it's also the key to connecting to that which inspires, motivates, or stimulates your target market. Those verbs are all essential in marketing, which at its core is about raising the awareness of a brand or product to stimulate interest, transition that interest into a valuable interaction, and share a vision with your audience.

How we connect emotionally to that which inspires and

stimulates others is very simple when we put the AAA strategy into practice:

Step 1. Get alignment.
Step 2. Take action.
Step 3. Prepare for adjustment.

First, we get aligned with those whom we are asking or attracting. In other words, we get aligned with our target market. To know what moves them, we have to know what their emotions and values are. Different things move people in different ways. If you are out of shape, you can be motivated by being marketed to with the emotions associated with getting you into shape. If you are poor, I can move you through your drive to be rich. If you are sick, I can move you by your desire to be well again. There are a whole range of emotions, especially attached to needs, wants, or goals, and we want to use that energy in motion to get aligned.

Ideally, we spend about 80 percent of our time getting alignment with the market. What does that mean? We're spending about 80 percent of our time determining the best way to connect emotionally with an audience. When we're connected emotionally, then we're aligned. One of the first steps to take is to look at the market and the emotions attached to the competing brands that make up your market. Investigate what the demographics of that market are.

Contemplate the foundational values of those in the market, determine whether those values are aligned with their core principles, and decide whether those values are components of their character, health, love, integrity, and/or some other aspect of their lives. Then, ask yourself what their experiential values are. What experiences do they value above others? If you love golf, then I can market to you using golfers or golf-themed content. That's the area where endorsements and sponsorships fall—all of them are directed toward that irrationality, the emotional attachment or alignment to a certain celebrity, athlete, or form of entertainment. We know that people can attach or be attracted emotionally to other people when they are aligned in the same values.

Using Kevin Hart to market its shoes, Nike can evoke an emotion of competitiveness, of redemption, of underdog turned hero, of elevation, of self-awareness—all of that, plus a bit of self-deprecation. Any number of emotions can be evoked, but in order to do so, we have to know *whom* we're aligning to and *what* emotion best aligns with them—and we do that either through those experiential values, or using what I call *giving values*.

We've all seen the Sarah McLachlan animal cruelty commercial and its strong emotional appeals. I feel like I give every time I see it because every time I see that puppy dog there, I'm pulled in by my love for the dogs I've had in my life and by my desire to help dogs in need. What do these commercials do? They've gotten alignment and emotional connection to my giving values. Why? When you see animals like the ones in the commercial, with those sad puppy eyes, looking like they're about to be put down, that's a big emotional pull. For just a dollar a day, you can save a suffering dog's life! That's a simple, impactful, emotional message. That's alignment. That's asking and attracting. That's marketing.

So how do we find out about the root of these emotional attachments? Apart from using research from outside sources, we can ask certain groups of people, or we can utilize hypothetical situations and see what emotions they attract. We also need to test marketing practices. With the popularity of social media, it is more important than ever to ask and to test the audience. You have more than 4.2 billion people to whom you can advertise to—and that number is ever growing.[1] With digital advertising tools, you can test the market to get a sense of what works, which means you can get aligned *before you take action*. That action that you take will have direct and quantitative results, and in marketing, it's key to tie our efforts to a quantitative result.

In the past, you could put out a newspaper ad to get alignment with a wide distribution of people. Traditionally, the only data that you could get from that ad was actual sales calls or leads. Then from there, you could convert some of those leads to sales, and you'd have that data. Now, we can gather a whole bunch of aligning data, even if people who view an online ad don't express a deep interest. We know whether they clicked on the ad or not. We know how long they stayed on the ad (if they did at all). And even though we don't know how truly interested they are, we do know the ad stimulated them to do something.

We can derive a mathematical equation or a return on investment knowing that data, and we can categorize that data and use it to hone our marketing skills. That is preparing for adjustment, the final A. We spend 80 percent of our time getting aligned emotionally with the audience we want to ask or attract. Then we take action and prepare for adjustment, and in today's world, the way we prepare for adjustment in offensive and defensive marketing is simply by gathering data and analyzing it to the best of our ability.

MAKE YOURSELF EQUAL, MAKE YOURSELF BETTER

The second part of offensive and defensive marketing is to know the vibration of what you're marketing and how that can resonate with your audience. Know your *product's* vibration, your *solution's* vibration, your *service's* vibration. Knowing what differentiates your solution, product, service, and self gives you an unmatched competitive advantage.

Notice I said "advantage." I didn't say anything about one thing being better than another. Why not? Because there are different vibrations. There are just certain things that attract certain people, connecting emotionally and aligning with their values. The same is true with the products, solutions, or services we market. And if things have a different vibration, the first thing we have to do in marketing, offensively in asking or defensively by attracting, is make ourselves *equal* to our competitors. This means identifying the ways that we are the same, whether we provide the same service, similar features, or solve the same problem. Then we must make ourselves different from competitors. We locate our audience's current perceptions to connect emotionally, then take it to a higher level by differentiating ourselves.

We can target a big audience when we understand the perception of the masses. When we are aligned with the emotions of others, we know how to better distinguish ourselves from other brands. We can find a competitive difference, which is something that all free agents in professional sports need to understand when they are trying to find another organization to take them on.

You can find examples of competitive differences being leveraged throughout all college and professional sports, but I think the best example comes from football. When college football players or rookies in the NFL first find themselves on a team, many are told one thing: special teams are the fastest way to get on the field. Special teams are an opportunity to have a competitive edge over the other players at your primary position, and that added value is something that teams covet, given their roster restrictions. And this is doubly true in the NFL, where teams have to deal with a salary cap.

Say you're an average wide receiver, for example. You can do everything that is asked of you as a wideout including running routes, catching, and blocking. You're equal to your competitors as a receiver. But if you have also shown an ability to return punts or kicks, or if you have experience serving as a "gunner"—the player who streaks down the sidelines on special teams plays in order to slow down the opponent's returner—you will have added value compared to other "average" players at your position. That's the example of how you make yourself equal and make yourself better.

What you want to do before leveraging your advantage is make yourself equal. You need to show that you possess the same attributes as your competitors, which means that you are equally deserving of consideration. Even to illuminate that similarity helps you in anything that you're doing, right? Illuminate the fact that you pretty much deliver the same thing as other free agent options in terms of receiving ability, while also possessing the added benefit of special teams skill and experience.

Pretend you're selling to a room of Coke lovers, and have Pepsi, when someone says "Well, I like Coca-Cola." What if I told them that Pepsi has the exact same ingredients and actually tastes the same as Coke? What if I told them that I'm going to switch the colors? What if I could convince all their friends to drink Pepsi? Would that make a difference in their perception? Probably. It's a *perception*.

Tastes or conditions or judgments are human constructs. And we have to understand that when we market, we can create that *perception*, or we can reengineer that perception by making ourselves equal, first, then by making ourselves different.

If you cannot convince people that you are equal to your competitors first, trying to convince them that you are uniquely differentiated becomes futile. If I'm Pepsi and I can't make myself equal to Coke, then it doesn't matter if I taste better. Your marketing plan and content should convey that your solution provides just as much value as the others, aligned with the emotions of others, while offering additional benefits or being different in some important way.

Let me show you on a personal level how that works. My company receives roughly 2,500 résumés a month, and the gist of what they say is this: "I want to work in sports. I'd like to work for you." The thing is, it's nearly impossible to distinguish, just by reading résumés, who is better than someone else and who among the applicants would be the better employees. So, the first thing we do, in order to decide whom we want to meet to take the conversation forward, is create a short list of résumés in which the applicants have somehow distinguished themselves. Everything else could be the same, could be equal. What we're looking for is *something*—a little something special—that gives a person distinguishing factor—an edge.

Knowing all the independent and dependent variables about you, your product, or your solution is the key to making yourself equal *and* making yourself different—that is, it's key to finding an "edge" you can exploit like a weakness in an opponent's defensive scheme. When you find the right vibration, you can deliver what other people do not expect from you. Nobody can argue with the highest truth. That frequency is inarguable.

GET YOUR REAR OFF THE BENCH

Laws of the Universe by which we should abide are simple: gratitude, empathy, accountability, and effective communication. But those laws are nothing without a secret weapon, the law of GOYA. John Assaraf, the New York Times best-selling author who was featured in the movie *The Secret*, taught me that you've got to *get off your ass*. I'm talking mentally, physically, and spiritually: get off your ass. Be consistent, persistent, and enjoy the pursuit of your potential. Make yourself equal, then make yourself different. Surprising people with those differences will give you the competitive advantage. You will have something different to offer, which will make people notice you.

When marketing yourself, a product, or service, the action you take is a critical component, whether you are pushing or pulling your audience. In terms of the AAA strategy, you simply cannot spend all of your time getting aligned with your target market. That would be like developing a game plan and then never putting it into practice.

Conversely, you should never believe your job is done when you take action. You need to analyze that action and its effectiveness, to better understand alternative options going forward. Adjustments to your plan are a crucial step as well, as very few game plans work perfectly the first time around. Your opponents and the market will adjust over time, and being prepared to make so-called half-time adjustments is another part of the law of GOYA. No player becomes an all-time great while sitting on the bench, and no coach creates a flawless game plan each and every contest, which is why it's important to take *all three steps*—alignment, action, and adjustment—not just one or two of them.

PUSH AND PULL MARKETING

Now, there's a big difference between *push marketing*, asking somebody, and *pull marketing*, attracting somebody. Pull marketing is meant to generate a demand for a product, and this is actually an attract. You are trying to attract consumers to try out your solution or to keep using the solutions. Push marketing, unlike pull marketing, is meant to sell out an existing supply of a product. It's a specific ask. I'm motivating or stimulating you with promotions, direct selling, negotiations, taste tests, packaging, and so on. Pull marketing is meant to generate a demand for a product. It's attracting with content like advertisements, campaigns, or stories that connect emotionally.

Both push and pull marketing efforts still have to connect emotionally to you. One's more aggressive than the other. If I'm pushing you to do something, I'm stimulating you to do it, whereas if I'm pulling you, I'm using the laws of attraction. It's much more obsequious to push someone than to pull him in. The approach I prefer favors the laws of attraction, allowing things to happen, attracting at the right vibration.

Even so, you don't get unless you ask, which for some of us can be a problem. We can attract all we want, but if we don't ask for what we want at some point, we won't get it. What happens so much of the time is that we do all the right things, but we don't have the awareness to see the opportunity in front of us, or we don't take advantage of it.

Although pushing and pulling aren't mutually exclusive,

the more people we pull, the better statistical success we'll have, in general. But we also use *bug lights*.

How do we use bug lights? Consider one of the retail events that grosses the most sales at Walmart: the release of the *Madden* game. The release date of *Madden* each year draws more people into Walmart than just about any other event besides the holidays. In fact, *Madden* was the item that sold the most online in the state of Montana for Walmart in 2017.[2] Walmart managers can use the appeal of the game as a bug light for their marketing. The game's release is a pull on consumers, one that can be leveraged through Walmart's various promotions for other products and services that are aligned with *Madden* purchasers, whether those are things like similar games or snacks to eat while playing. Now if there are no asks, these managers would diminish the effectiveness of their marketing capacity. Asks are things that stimulate or compel you to buy, whereas pulls are things that stimulate or attract your interest.

BELIEVE IN YOUR VALUE

None of this matters—*none of it*—unless you are confident enough to ask, and there is one limiting belief, an energetic flaw, that many of us have which causes us to defer. This is a feeling that we are somehow not worthy. That's why the 100/20 Rule, mentioned in Chapter 2, is so important in your life. Think about getting a stack of a hundred $100 bills and being told that you will receive a commission each time you trade one of those $100 bills for a $20 bill. How long will it take you to get rid of that stack? How would you feel while you were giving away $10,000 worth of value and asking for only $2,000 back? I can't imagine it would take you much time to give away a hundred $100 bills and get a hundred $20 bills back.

Imagine taking that same mindset with your marketing approach and doing that every day. Imagine carrying a belief that the value you are providing others is much greater than what you are asking in return. That relationship is a subtlety of success, and with that belief, the only time failure occurs is when we're not asking.

Look in your sent box in your email at the end of a workday and see how many people you actually asked for help. I guarantee you offered help to someone, so contemplate why you didn't give others the gift of asking for their assistance. The most basic, beneficial ask that you can have is, "Excuse me, can you help me, or do you know someone else who can?" A vast majority of the people you ask will say, "Yes, what can I do for you?" or direct you to someone who can help.

And the small percentage who don't react positively tend to be people that you don't want to mess with anyway.

POSTGAME WRAP-UP

You need to understand the difference between push and pull, but more than the difference between push and pull, you need to understand the value of pulling somebody in through attraction and closing them by asking. Some people skip the attraction stage, but I propose to you that the offensive and defensive marketing principles are not mutually exclusive.

You need offense as well as defense to win the marketing game, just as you need both components to win any team sport. You cannot just attract. And you cannot just pull.

The offensive and defensive aspects of marketing are a matter of getting people to align, take action, and prepare for adjustment, understanding your vibrations so you can make yourself equal, then make yourself different. Always connect emotionally not only to others but also to that which inspires them, stimulates them, and motivates them.

Finally, understand the nonmutual exclusivity of push and pull marketing. You can attract whomever you like, but unless you are confident enough in the value you hold to ask, you are never going to get anything in return.

8

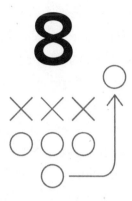

The Offense
and Defense of
Communication

PREGAME ANALYSIS

When it comes to communication, there is one overarching goal: get your point across as clearly as possible when you are connecting with other people. This is how you make sure your message is conveyed and your team is aligned with your team goals and your overarching values. In this chapter, you will learn not only how to get your point across clearly but also how to ask the right questions to better connect with those around you.

There are three distinct keys to any interpersonal communication. Those are what content you choose to convey, the access you provide to that content, and the medium through which you choose to express the content. Failure to select the right content, access, or medium is a nemesis of effective communication. That is why you need to elevate your awareness by paying close attention to the *way* you connect to others and by understanding *whom* you are connecting to. Just as important as what you say is the person listening, so learn to understand what type of listener you are dealing with (which I will define later in the chapter) in order to avoid frustration and wasting your energy or time.

People use emotions in conjunction with logical reasons to make a decision, which is why tapping into their emotions is an essential part of sharing your vision. Often, we focus on only one purpose of communication, communicating directly with others for some sort of gain, and we neglect one of the best ways to connect emotionally: communicating with that which inspires us. That inspiration brings clarity to our communication, and clarity gives us confidence to take action.

Learning to ask the right questions, both open-ended and close-ended, also brings clarity, and this is a major component in effective communication. When you understand the roles of emotion and inspiration in communication, when you know how to clarify the thoughts of others and get alignment, and when you know how to select the right way to communicate your value to other people, you'll have the communication skills of a champion. And those skills will empower you to win, whether you are sharing a message with others or taking in their message.

COMMUNICATING A VISION

Sharing a vision is the essential part of communication because sharing a vision means that we both share one mind when it comes to the goals we set, and the actions necessary to get there, which means we're connected. This shared vision comes from sharing the value you bring to the table with others clearly and concisely, in a way that connects others emotionally to that value. When we share one mind, we're able to collaborate and create a greater collective belief, with all of our team members connected to the same pursuit.

The core component of any team, whether it's in business or sports, is that collective belief or shared vision of what we desire to achieve together. If we all share the same values with which to pursue those goals, like gratitude, empathy, accountability, and effective communication, then we're able to make decisions based on the same criteria. In other words, when we come to the point of sharing a vision, our team members are moving forward together, toward a shared vision, and we don't have to waste additional time training people in what or how to communicate with those inside their organization.

Emotional connection, more than facts or logic, is at the heart of true effective communication. If team members are not connected or we don't share a vision, we don't know what "play" we're running. When that is the situation, we're never going to win. "Playground football," devoid of any strategy, will always lose against a well-coached team with a proper scheme or plan. And if we don't have shared values and goals, then we're all running different plays. If a catcher and pitcher aren't on the same page with the signals used to call for pitches, the batter has a massive advantage. Don't let your lack of a shared vision impair your ability to score!

These connection problems happen all the time. It's why people fail in their business and personal relationships, and it's why they fail to reach their objectives—because they have forgotten the simplest rule, which is that people buy on emotion or connect on emotion for logical reasons. Effective communication is needed to develop expectations between you and your clients, subordinates, or compatriots, and it is needed to then manage those expectations going forward.

THE TWO WAYS TO CONNECT AND COMMUNICATE

We want to have everyone on our team on the same page, so that we're prepared to execute on the plan. Getting on the same page is foremost about establishing the connection between your team members, which happens in two different ways.

We first establish a connection by emotionally connecting to one person or a group. My speaking, for example, has improved tremendously not just onstage but in video and in audio too because my intent is to connect emotionally. It's not only *what* I say. It's *how* I say it. I'm connecting emotionally when I'm talking about the things that are important to me, whether it is about being more interested than interesting or taking advice the way you would pick up a handful of sand. Look, I've been teaching these same lessons for decades. So why haven't they become tired? Because I believe deeply in the values I'm imparting, and I've learned to connect emotionally through those stories I tell to reinforce those values, and that emotion resonates with those around me.

The second way to communicate is to connect to that which inspires you, whatever that may be. Part of effective communication is connecting to that which inspires you because inspiration is the fuel for your action. It's the fuel that goes through you to others. Inspiration allows us to do things that we can't even fathom doing. If you are inspired, time becomes a supernatural construct, not a natural construct. The axiom "Time flies when you're having fun" perfectly illustrates this relationship. Time is once again hard to determine when you're inspired, but human-made time is very easy to determine by just looking at a clock, watch, or smartphone.

Many times, our views or the views of others can be obscured by our not fully understanding the role of time and ego in decision making. We perceive some shortage, obstacle, or difference between us and those we are trying to communicate with (such as inferiority or superiority), and we use that as an excuse to not communicate at all (we shut down or close ourselves off). That is why it is so important to be aligned with our audience and to align our message with the values of those we are targeting, so we can be as clear as possible when we are talking or listening to others.

CLARITY IN COMMUNICATION

Communication expert Frank Luntz used to say, "It's not what you say. It's what people hear."[1] To me, that's the crux of emotional communication. So many times, we perceive what others are saying factually and logically, but yet we're not connected emotionally. This can result in somebody's hearing the complete opposite of what we're intending to say. This happens all too often. To avoid this issue, when we're directing our team, our family, or our community, when we're calling a play, we want to be fast, clear, and concise.

Jon Gruden, who's now back to coaching in the NFL, was notorious for lengthy play verbiage. He had an episode of his *Quarterback Camp* show with quarterback Cam Newton in which he talked about the difference between simplified college offenses, like the one Newton ran at Auburn, and the plays that are called in the NFL. He mentioned to Newton that there were shifts, protections, snap counts, alerts, the "check with me" instructions, and all sorts of other components of the play that needed to be expressed in a play call. In his complicated pro-style offense, Gruden would make the play call, "Flip right, double X, jet, 36 counter naked waglet, seven X quarter."[2] When he reentered the NFL as the

Raiders' head coach, Jon realized that he needed to be more effective in the way that he communicated, simplifying his verbiage in order to make things easier on the team.

You need to clearly communicate after you have established an emotional connection. You need to know the vibration or understanding or awareness that your team members have. One of my best employees ever was originally from China. He could execute just about any plan, despite the fact that English was not his first language. In fact, because he didn't know English as fluently as the rest of the team, he was always extremely focused on making sure he repeated exactly what I told him to tell others, and *how* I said it, and that resulted in his having success with the pitch. Another area this employee excelled in was getting clarification, as he was always more interested than interesting, and he chose to communicate effectively by asking at least one more question to ensure that he understood what was being said. In communication, being more interested than interesting is a state of curiosity, where you are eager to learn from and gain alignment with others.

Questioning is very important in communication because it brings clarity. We've all experienced a time when we didn't ask questions during a conversation, and then we had to call the person back to ask him or her for clarification. Getting clarification and/or confirmation of what you believe is essential to create a strong connection or alignment. We cannot let the ego get in the way. We need to be accountable for getting the right information.

Lou Holtz, legendary Notre Dame football coach, said, "I've never learned anything talking. I only learn things when I ask questions."[3] When we ask questions to clarify the communication and we are more interested than interesting, we gain better alignment with those around us.

Now, there are two types of questions to ask to get alignment and share a vision, the first being *open-ended questions*. The reason we ask open-ended questions first is to connect emotionally to another. When trying to learn more about another's business, for example, a very common open-ended question to start with is, "What do you do today?" On-topic, open-ended questions will connect you emotionally in almost any situation: "What do you do today?" "What do you like about it?" "What don't you like about it?"

I know this sounds simple, and yet most people find it surprisingly difficult to put into practice. This is not rocket science. This is simplicity. Think about it this way: the best open-ended questions are meant to gain as much information as possible about people's values and how they relate to a given task or opportunity.

Open-ended questions are normally asked when starting to get alignment. The overall goal of asking open-ended questions is to get **stable data** in order to make an informed decision, but even more importantly, it allows you to emotionally connect to others or to that which inspires others. Stable data has no statistical noise or unnecessary information. It is simply a set of well-informed data points with which you can make a decision.

STABLE DATA: A set of correct information that enables us and empowers us to make the right calls.

How do we get stable data? Ask open-ended questions. The more we're aware of what's occurring around us, the more accurate decisions we will make. If we knew as a defensive coordinator, for example, what play the other team was going to run, if we had an awareness, we would have a much higher rate of statistical success stopping that team. If I were a hitter who knew what pitch was coming from a pitcher who was tipping his pitches, I would have better data, and my decisions would yield better results. One touch of awareness—simply by being more interested than interesting, connecting emotionally, asking open-ended questions, and getting stable data to raise your awareness or certainty of what's going to happen—is a boon to you when making any call.

Without stable data, we cannot make consistent or accurate calls. How do we know if data is stable? Once we've connected emotionally, then we can qualify the data that we're given. How do we do that? Consider the credibility of the source. Credibility of the source in communication is so important, both as someone who's giving data and receiving data. We might have historical analysis that allows us to say, "That source is likely to be credible (or not)." However, the most important, most credible of all sources is that which inspires us, as truth is inspiring.

OK, so now we have stable data. Then what? Now we have to ask *close-ended questions*. These are questions we use after open-ended questions so we can establish more logical alignment on top of our preexisting emotional connection.

I'll give you examples of close-ended questions. Let's just say I'm selling customer relationship management (CRM) software and competing against Salesforce. I could start by asking open-ended questions such as, "What do you use today? What do you like about it? What don't you like about it?" Then I could ask a close-ended question such as, "What if I were able to give you this particular functionality that you like, combined with this back-end support and this unique offering? Would you be interested?" A close-ended question usually has a yes or no answer. When you give me the yes answer, I'm allowing you to take my ideas and make them yours. The more close-ended questions that I can get you to agree with so as to align your values with mine, the better the connection, both logical and emotional, we can establish. At the end of this dialogue, I would ask you one key question: "Can you see any reason that you wouldn't want to move forward with my CRM tool?"

Emotional connections are very simple. They're based on what you like or what you don't like, what makes you happy or sad. Those are the basic emotions at the center of connection. Every other emotion can be tied to those basic emotions. Frustration, anger, and all of the ego-based feelings are manifestations of those basic emotions.

An emotional connection is as simple as this: "It makes me feel good." I can provide customers more of what they like and fix what they don't like to make them happy, which is providing them value. This allows me to have statistical success and to share a vision, defined in this chapter as communicating or connecting.

You cannot connect emotionally to others unless you know what they don't like or like, or how something makes them feel. And to understand their feelings, there are only two types of questions that you ask: open- and close-ended questions. From there, there is only one process to confirm that you've shared a vision: ask them if the way that you've connected makes them feel comfortable and aligned. Then you can give them the logical reasons and facts and capabilities to give your product or service more value than what they're getting from what they're currently using, or more value to make them feel good, because it's all relative.

MASTERING COMMUNICATIONS CONTENT, ACCESS, AND MEDIA

There are three basic components you need to utilize in order to communicate properly with those around you, which I previously discussed in Chapter 6. First off is the **content**: what is being communicated. Content includes verbal and nonverbal communication that connects us with other people through our conscious, subconscious, and unconscious mind. It's *what* the content is, the message that is being shared, that connects us.

> **CONTENT:** What you communicate with others. This shared message is generally tied to an emotional pull of some sort.

Sometimes we need to adjust our content for the audience that we have. Often, we need to take emotion out of the communication when dealing with different calls, meetings, or interviews. We cannot allow our ego, which includes fears and deadline pressures, to create unnecessary resistances, shortages, voids, or obstacles. The content that we have has to be void of our ego, with no need to be right, offended, fearful, guilty, or anything else. All of the needs of the ego are obstacles to connecting emotionally, and if we can't connect emotionally, then we can't truly share our content.

Content can be ideas or words, and they can be written or presented in video or audio form. Content can be shared in many different ways, but no matter which way, the key thing is to make it connect emotionally.

How do we do that? By utilizing the second component: **access**. Accessibility goes two ways: with those around you as well as with what inspires you. We have to be accessible to others, meaning we have to be able to communicate to others, and we have to be accessible to help others. Be of service! Content is, in general, engineered to be accessible to others, but we also have to be able to access inspiration, or data, or content ourselves. *Nothing* just originates in you. If it did, then everything would be happening to you and you alone. So, we need to be able to access content, and we need to make ourselves accessible.

ACCESS: The methods by which you connect to necessary information and to that which inspires you.

Think about information, data, or content in terms of X. When I receive it, X becomes *X plus David.* And then it goes out to another person, at which point it becomes *X plus David plus that person*, and it keeps going as the content advances, like the game of "telephone" you played when you were a child. That's access, and with the prevalence of information today it's more important than ever to understand and be efficient, effective, and statistically successful at accessing information than it is to simply know the information itself.

That was not always true. When I was young, it was important for me to remember the 50 states, for me to study and remember equations and theories and all of those things. But it makes no sense at today's vibration to spend my time focusing on simply knowing certain things when I already know how to *access* them. The way we function has evolved to a state of knowing how to get the answer, as opposed to simply knowing the answer, because in today's world we possess a handheld brain.

So, why are you focusing or spending your time being redundant if you have a handheld brain that tends to be more accurate than our memory, in general, and is able to access information better than our human capabilities would ever allow us? Ask yourself, "What am I better able to do than my wireless devices can do?" The answer is simple: you can communicate and connect emotionally. That smartphone can't connect emotionally, but it *can* access data and information better than you can. I promise, it can access information better than every single one of us. It no longer makes sense to try to amass vast stores of knowledge. It makes better sense to master access to that information and capitalize on your unique capabilities: forging meaningful, emotional connections.

We've always had content. Nowadays people will tell you content is king. Why? Because the truth vibrates the fastest, and the best ideas stick around. They are perpetual. My classic example is Mickey Mouse. Mickey Mouse was a great idea when he was whistling on a steamboat drawn in black-and-white on flip cards. Today, the Mickey Mouse channel has had more than 2 billion views on YouTube.[4] This is pretty much the exact same idea and content as the original; it's just more accessible.

Great ideas perpetuate, which is why access today may be more important than great ideas. In the past, if you wanted a great idea, there were two ways to get it. Literally, you had to physically manifest it yourself, or memorize it, and then reaccess it. Today you don't have to do either, thanks to digital technology that allows you to access so much more information and data than you could ever comprehend. Today you're spending your time figuring out, "How do I input the right things to get the right data?" "How do I make the right ask?" "What is the right research?"

One of the things that I won't do is memorize information because the handheld brain has a greater capacity and better efficiency. Why waste my resources? I'd much rather develop other parts of my brain that allow me to connect emotionally and to access inspiration—in other words, do things the handheld brain can't do. Accessing and sharing information shifts our communication from offensive to defensive. When we're accessing the information instead of memorizing, we're on the defensive.

Now, one of the most critical business tasks out there is clarifying data. There's too much data, too many people. Cleaning data is the defensive part of communication. If you want to figure out and spend your time memorizing what's available to you on your handheld brain, go ahead. But I would suggest that it's not information that's key. It's access. If you don't focus on access, you can have all the information in the world, and you're still not going to have the right answers.

The third and final component of effective communication is the **medium**. This is where we communicate, the method of communication in which content is presented, which allows us (and our ideas) both access and accessibility. The number of mediums grows and grows and grows. That's why choosing the right medium for our communication is just as important as the content and access we choose.

> **MEDIUM:** The location or method with which you access or share content with other individuals.

Different business situations, just like different plays called in a game, require different mediums of communication. If we watch a football game, for example, many college football teams, like the aforementioned Auburn Tigers, now have these big cards with funny logos, signs, and pictures to communicate. Coaches also have wireless devices to communicate. The people on the sideline also have hand signals to communicate. They also have pats on the bottoms to communicate. They also raise their hands in celebration, or hang their heads in defeat.

Those are all mediums, but all types of media address a different vibration or use a different way to communicate, and they all appeal to different audiences. In business, when is a phone call appropriate? When should we use email? When should we text? How should we use the different social media platforms, such as Instagram, YouTube, Facebook, Snapchat, LinkedIn, and Twitter? Can we use them all? I say you should use all types of communication media—in person, on the phone, via email, and all forms of social media—but you should prioritize those media that give you the best access.

One of the best examples of access I've found came from dealing with my mother. The most valuable thing in her life is her grandchildren. To be accessible to them and for them to be accessible to her is what makes her life worthwhile. She also is a third-degree black belt in Jewish guilt who regularly calls me and tells me that my three teenage daughters don't love her.

Well, of course they love her, and I told her so. Her reply? "Well, they don't call me." I told her that expecting teenagers to call you is like expecting great Chinese food at a Nouvelle Cuisine French restaurant. It's just not on the menu.

My advice to her? Learn to use Snapchat.

My mom's initial response: "I can't learn Snapchat."

I said, "What are you talking about, you can't learn Snapchat? You can learn Snapchat in six minutes."

She said, "Oh, I couldn't do that. How do you know I could learn it in six minutes?"

To which I replied, "Because my six-year-old son taught me in six minutes!"

We create resistance in our own lives because we don't have stable data, and then we don't get what we want because we're not using the right medium to access the content we want. The content that my mom wanted? Love from her grandchildren. The access that she wanted? To be accessible and to access what was going on in their lives, to connect emotionally to that which is most important to her. That wasn't happening, not because of intention, attention, or effort, but because of the medium.

With this example, you see how people have to connect emotionally and how important content, access, and mediums all are in effective communication. If the mediums you select are getting in the way of that connection, or not allowing access to content, you will never build a strong connection to those around you—without which you cannot have meaningful communication.

LEARN ABOUT LISTENERS

None of what I've said about communication matters if we don't understand our listeners. There are three types of listeners in the world.

First is what I like to call the *interrupters*. The interrupters are people who, when you're talking to them and trying to connect emotionally, make it impossible. All they're worried about is telling you what *they* think. They desire control over the conversation. Their desire to share their own content while ignoring yours results in your not being able to connect emotionally.

The second type of listeners are the *waiters*. The waiters just can't wait to tell you what they think. The entire time you're talking to them, that's all they're thinking about. They don't care what you're saying, and it is impossible for you to connect emotionally to them because they are thinking only about what they want to tell you. These first two types of listeners have their egos in the way, which interferes with any attempt you make to connect.

Then, finally, there are the **transformative listeners**. Transformative listeners are people you can connect to emotionally. You pass on your content in order to empower them to access it, and then they, in turn, make it accessible to others. They connect with what you're saying on an emotional level, and then they can share it and emotionally connect with others. In this way, there can be a complete emotional connection with no ego-based blockages. That's truly effective communication.

> **TRANSFORMATIVE LISTENERS:** People who not only emotionally connect to and comprehend the ideas that are shared but who are also able to transform those ideas by adding their own valuable insights and easily share them with others.

The Boston Celtics head coach, Brad Stevens, is a young coach renowned for his ability to lead his teams, especially through the power of effective communication. Brad Stevens certainly doesn't know the most about basketball. There are countless basketball coaches who have coached longer than he's been involved in basketball. They've seen more plays and they have more situation knowledge, relationship capital, and expertise in the game of basketball.

Communication is one of the keys to Brad's success. His communication style may not be groundbreaking, but it is extremely effective. According to a 2018 *Boston Business Journal* article, he advocates for an open line of communication between all members of an organization, and he doesn't limit communication to just basketball.[5] He has created an environment in which people feel free to share what is important to them and everyone's perspectives are valuable, heard, and connected to emotionally.

Brad Stevens is a transformative leader, a transformative person. He is also a transformative listener, and that's what has created his exponential success at such a young age. He advocates for the two Cs: being *concise* and being *candid*. Being concise is being clear; being candid is speaking the truth. With those simple but effective goals in mind, he's achieved stellar results and is the type of leader you can build a team around.

POSTGAME WRAP-UP

When it comes to making any call, your team should be able to turn a simple call into execution. If things seem too complex, that means you're not communicating effectively, and in order to communicate in an offensive and defensive way, you need to make sure that you have the best content and you have proper access to it, utilizing the right media.

Like the fast-paced college offenses that use a system of images on signs to quickly call plays from the sidelines, the simpler the play call, the readier your team will be to execute it. You want to make sure that you have alignment with your team members by first asking open-ended questions and making that emotional connection, and then asking close-ended questions.

Even more importantly, summarize the content that you share so you know what you said is the same as what your listener heard.

It's not what we say. It's how we say it. So be a transformative communicator, and let things come through you.

Take shared content, add your insights and experiences to it, and make your communication clear and concise for others. When you are confident enough to share your vision, you can empower others to communicate effectively, and then empower others to do the same.

Quick Play Guide

B elow are some quick "plays" for you to follow in order to hone your decision-making skills and empower yourself and your team to thrive and win—all while staying grounded in the consistent and persistent pursuit of your potential as a leader.

Putting Together Your Roster
by Building Yourself (Chapter 1)

o When it comes to attracting the right team to you, first look at the core values that you will rally your team around. Teams that are aligned in their values are always more likely to accomplish their goals than teams that aren't.

○ Next, look into your repetitive thoughts, and identify the thoughts and patterns that are harming your ability to make quick and accurate decisions. Effective leaders understand how to manage their rosters, cutting those members whose production does not match up with the resources dedicated to them.

○ Finally, manage your relationships just as you manage your "thought roster." Learn to cut those individuals who drain you, and provide your energy to those people who energize you instead.

Offensive/Defensive Mindset (Chapter 2)

○ Your mind can be your greatest weapon and biggest vulnerability, so put an initial focus on the positive and negative thought patterns that you can identify. It is especially vital to look at the tasks you can excel at without much thought—in other words, your unconscious competencies.

○ Another susceptibility you need to look at is the repetitive (negative) self-talk you might be engaging in. When you can counter this negative self-talk, you will be able to build a better roster of conscious and subconscious thoughts.

○ Finally, take a look at the way you respond to slumps and mistakes. Living in accountability and pursuing progress

instead of perfection will empower you to deal with anything that comes your way.

Coaching Trees and Growth (Chapter 3)

o Mentorship is one of the fastest ways to learn and grow,
no matter what business you are in. Position yourself to
learn from three individuals who sit in a position you
want to be in, and position others in your organization to
connect with and learn from mentors as well.

o Humility is a major factor in any successful mentor-mentee
relationship. Be radically humble enough to ask others for
help because other people can help you avoid paying the
dummy tax that they have already paid themselves.

o One of the best ways to foster personal and professional
growth is simply to live with an energy of forgiveness.
Forgiveness cancels out any fear of failing you might have,
and that fear will never again paralyze you from taking
action.

Don't Trip on the First-Down Chains
Behind You (Chapter 4)

o In order to have a well-rounded perspective on the
past, present, and future, you should take time to study
human nature and the emotions associated with it. In
this way, you will elevate your awareness in order to lever-

age human nature and emotional appeals in the actions you take.

o Practice identifying the times when you are in your comfort zone, learning zone, and anxiety zone. When you understand how habitual actions make you feel, you can expand your comfort zone, spend more time in the learning zone, and reduce the tasks that give you anxiety.

o Finally, practice dealing with the missteps and mistakes you make along the way with gratitude, empathy, accountability, and effective communication. When you have an appropriate mistake response, you can take rapid corrective action without undue bias or negative emotional impacts.

Being in the Game (Chapter 5)

o Being present in the moment is essential when making decisions, but often something happens to throw us off our game. When you understand that you will always experience highs and lows, you can maintain a perspective that keeps you pushing forward.

o Consistency is something that we all strive for, no matter what aspect of skills, knowledge, or desires we are working on improving. When we can lower the bar in order to build and maintain consistency, we will avoid "zeroing out" any progress that we make.

o One of the biggest struggles for top decision makers comes from an inability to detach their happiness or self-worth from the outcomes of their decisions. When you can consistently detach from the outcomes, without losing sight of your goals, you will always be in the game.

The Offense and Defense
of Branding (Chapter 6)

o In order to brand anything, you first need to pay attention to its emotional appeal because consumers buy on emotion for logical reasons. When you find a frequency that resonates with consumers, you can better spread your messaging.

o When it comes to the messages you send others to build a brand, you must know when to *ask* and when to *attract* your customers. This means understanding the right content, access, and mediums with which to share those messages with others.

o The best way to brand a person, product, or company comes from utilizing the *stage theory* with consistency. This means capturing content that is aligned authentically with your brand and then amplifying and perpetuating those messages with the right mediums.

The Offense and Defense of Marketing (Chapter 7)

o In order to make the most of your marketing efforts, employ the *AAA strategy*. Take the time to get *alignment* with your target market, take appropriate *action*, and then prepare to *adjust*.

o When competing in a dog-eat-dog marketplace, you need to find a way to successfully compare yourself to your competitors. First, identify the ways that you are similar to or equal to your competition, and then showcase the differences and competitive advantages you have over others.

o Finally, your marketing efforts all need to carry an energy or underlying theme of value. Build your confidence that you are providing $100 of value and asking for only $20 in return in order to convey effectively that message to others.

The Offense and Defense of Communication (Chapter 8)

o Practice the two ways to communicate, with those around you as well as with what inspires you. When you are able to tap into inspiration, you are then able to share that energy and passion with others and empower the team around you to win.

○ Focus on being clear and concise when sharing a vision with others. When your team clearly hears and understands the direction you give, they are able to execute it.

○ Communication is most effective when you understand the type of listeners that you are dealing with. Evaluate those around you, and remind them to appreciate the conversations you are having, so they can add value to the messages that are shared instead of just taking in those messages.

Endnotes

CHAPTER 1: Putting Together Your Roster by Building Yourself

1. Sigmund Freud, *Civilization and Its Discontents*
2. *Life of Reason, Reason in Society*, Scribner's, 1905, p. 35
3. *Tischreden (Table Talk)* (1569), Martin Luther
4. "Jerry West Quotes," *BrainyQuote*, https://www.brainyquote.com/authors/jerry_west.

CHAPTER 2: Offensive/Defensive Mindset

1. Paul Slovic, "Behavioral Problems of Adhering to a Decision Policy," unpublished manuscript, 1973, https://www.cia.gov/library/center-for-the-study-of-intelligence/csi-publications/books-and-monographs/psychology-of-intelligence-analysis/art8.html.

CHAPTER 3: Coaching Trees and Growth

1. Kevin Hong, "Struggling to Succeed? Use the Strategy That Earned Kobe Bryant an Oscar Nomination (Seriously)," *Inc.*, January 26, 2018, https://www.inc.com/kevin-hong/kobe-bryant-received-an-oscar-nomination-proving-every-entrepreneur-should-ask-for-help-more-often.html.

2. Bill Russell, "We Are Nothing Without Our Mentors," *USA TODAY*, January 20, 2016, https://www.usatoday.com/story/sports/nba/2016/01/20/bill-russell-boston-celtics-mentor/79057628/.

3. https://www.apnews.com/fd388899c7524ca5988416d7923230bb

4. Associated Press, "Coaching Lesson No. 1 from Bill Parcells: Give Your Team the Best Chance to Win," *Fox News Sports*, July 28, 2013, https://www.foxnews.com/sports/coaching-lesson-no-1-from-bill-parcells-give-your-team-the-best-chance-to-win.

5. "Bill Parcells Quotes," *AZ Quotes*, from Bill Parcells and Nunyo Demasio, *Parcells: A Football Life* (New York: Crown Archetype, 2014), https://www.azquotes.com/author/11297-Bill_Parcells.

CHAPTER 4: Don't Trip on the First-Down Chains Behind You

1. https://www.kansascity.com/sports/spt-columns-blogs/for-petes-sake/article187034303.html

2. *Nike Culture: The Sign of the Swoosh* (1998), by Robert Goldman and Stephen Papson, p. 49

CHAPTER 5: Being in the Game

1. https://www.heraldnet.com/sports/jordan-makes-comeback
   -official-to-sign-with-wizards-for-two-years/
2. "Henry Ford Quotes," *Goodreads*, https://www.goodreads.com
   /author/quotes/203714.Henry_Ford.
3. Bill Murphy, Jr., "Want to Be Luckier? Here's How the Founder
   of McDonald's Said He Increased His Own Good Luck,"
   Inc., January 4, 2018, https://www.inc.com/bill-murphy-jr
   /mcdonalds-founder-heres-how-to-make-your-own-luck.html.
4. Robert McG. Thomas, Jr., "Orville Redenbacher, Famous for
   His Popcorn, Is Dead at 88," *New York Times*, September 20,
   1995, https://www.nytimes.com/1995/09/20/obituaries/orville
   -redenbacher-famous-for-his-popcorn-is-dead-at-88.html.

CHAPTER 7: The Offense and Defense of Marketing

1. *Internet World Stats*, "Internet Users in the World by Regions,"
   2018 Population Stats, https://www.internetworldstats.com
   /stats.htm.
2. Tribune Media Wire, "Walmart Reveals Top Selling Items
   Sold Online in Each State in 2017," *News 3 TV*, WTKR, Nor-
   folk, VA, December 28, 2017, https://wtkr.com/2017/12/28
   /walmart-reveals-top-selling-items-sold-online-in-each-state
   -in-2017/.

CHAPTER 8: The Offense and Defense of Communication

1. Ruth Sherman, "Leadership: 'It's Not What You Say, It's What
   People Hear'—Frank Luntz," *Fast Company*, September 24, 2007,
   https://www.fastcompany.com/660890/leadership-its-not
   -what-you-say-its-what-people-hear-frank-luntz.

2. Transcribed from "Video: Gruden's QB Camp—Cam Newton," *NFL Nation*, ESPN, http://www.espn.com/blog/nfcnorth
   /post/_/id/25861/video-grudens-qb-camp-cam-newton.
3. "Lou Holtz Quotes," *Goodreads*, https://www.goodreads.com
   /author/quotes/85179.Lou_Holtz.
4. Micky Mouse YouTube Channel, "Disney Shorts: About,"
   https://www.youtube.com/user/DisneyShorts/about.
5. Joe Halpern, "Holding Court: Celtics Coach Brad Stevens
   Shares His Management Philosophy," *Boston Business Journal/
   Bizjournals*, August 8, 2018, https://www.bizjournals.com
   /boston/news/2018/08/08/holding-court-celtics-coach-brad
   -stevens-shares.html.

Index

About the Author

David Meltzer is CEO of Sports 1 Marketing, one of the world's most successful sports marketing firms, and has been recognized as "Sports Humanitarian of the Year" by *Variety*. He has spent 25 years working as an entrepreneur and executive in the legal, technology, sports, and entertainment fields.